A CONCISE
EXEGETICAL
GRAMMAR

of

NEW TESTAMENT GREEK

J. Harold Greenlee, Ph. D.
Professor of New Testament Greek
Asbury Theological Seminary
Wilmore, Kentucky

Wm. B. Eerdmans Publishing Company
Grand Rapids, Michigan

PHOTOLITHOPRINTED BY CUSHING - MALLOY, INC.
ANN ARBOR, MICHIGAN, UNITED STATES OF AMERICA
1963

Preface

This booklet is intended to meet the needs of students who have completed a course in elementary New Testament Greek. Its purpose is to give a grasp of the principles of grammar which are meaningful in exegesis.

These principles are intentionally presented in concise form. The aim of the book is to be practical, not exhaustive. Minor exceptions to rules are for the most part not presented. For the student who wishes to investigate a point more fully, references to other grammars are given throughout.

The author trusts that this booklet, by giving students an unsophisticated presentation of principles, will encourage many in the practice of "rightly dividing the word of truth."

Table of Contents

ETYMOLOGY

SYNTAX

A CONCISE EXEGETICAL GRAMMAR
OF
NEW TESTAMENT GREEK

The task of exegetical grammar is to enable the interpreter to reproduce in his own mind the exact thought of each given form or expression in the Greek New Testament, and then to express that thought, as nearly as possible, in his own language. Bu 2-5.

Abbreviations used

Bu   Burton, Ernest DeWitt: Syntax of the Moods and Tenses in New Testament Greek

DM   Dana, H. E., and Julius R. Mantey: A Manual Grammar of the Greek New Testament

Gr   Green, Samuel G.: Handbook to the Grammar of the Greek Testament, rev. ed.

Ma   Machen, J. Gresham: New Testament Greek for Beginners

Me   Metzger, Bruce M.: Lexical Aids for Students of New Testament Greek

Mo   Moulton, J. H.: Grammar of New Testament Greek. Vol. I, Prolegomena

MH   Moulton, J. H., and W. F. Howard: Grammar of New Testament Greek. Vol II, Accidence and Word-Formation

Nu   Nunn, H. P. V., Short Syntax of New Testament Greek

Ro   Robertson, A. T.: A Grammar of the Greek New Testament in the Light of Historical Research

RD   Robertson, A. T., and W. H. Davis: A New Short Grammar of the Greek Testament

References in Green are to sections; in all others, to pages. The Greek text is that of the 17th edition of Nestle.

ETYMOLOGY

I. The alphabet. Gr #1; Ma 1; DM 20; MH 37

A. Lower case

α β γ δ ε ζ η θ ι κ λ μ ν ξ ο

π ρ σ (ς) τ υ φ χ ψ ω

B. Capitals

Α Β Γ Δ Ε Ζ Η Θ Ι Κ Λ Μ Ν Ξ Ο

Π Ρ Σ Τ Υ Φ Χ Ψ Ω

II. Vowels and diphthongs. Gr #3; Ma 10–11

A. Vowels   α ε η ι ο υ ω
Long: η ω
Short: ε ο
Long or short: α ι υ

B. Diphthongs

αι	αυ	ᾳ	ηυ
ει	ευ	ῃ	ωυ
οι	ου	ῳ	
υι			

C. A long syllable is a syllable containing a long vowel or a diphthong.
Exception: When the diphthongs αι or οι are the last two letters of a word, they are considered short for purposes of accenting when the accent falls on some other syllable.

III. Transliteration. Me 3, 98–101; Gr #7

A. Letters
Most transliterations of single letters are obvious, but the following may be mentioned:

1. η - long e   υ - y (not u)
    κ - c (usually)   χ - ch (not k)
    ξ - x

2. ι may become j. Initial ρ, which always has a rough breathing, usually becomes rh.

B. Diphthongs

$\alpha\iota$ - <u>ae</u> or <u>e</u> $\varepsilon\iota$ - <u>e</u> or <u>i</u>
$o\iota$ - <u>oe</u> or <u>e</u> $o\upsilon$ - <u>u</u>

IV. Accents. Ma 13-18 (especially 14), 44-45

 A. General rules

  1. The <u>acute</u> accent can stand on one of the last three syllables.
   The <u>circumflex</u> can stand on one of the last two syllables.
   An acute accent standing on an ultima is replaced by a <u>grave</u> accent when other words follow in the sentence without intervening punctuation.

  2. If the ultima is long, the acute accent may stand on one of the last two syllables only, and the circumflex on the last syllable only.

  3. The circumflex may stand on long syllables only.

  4. When the penult (last syllable but one) is to be accented, if it is long and the ultima is short the accent on the penult must be a circumflex.

 B. <u>Verb</u> accent is recessive--i.e., the accent is placed as far from the ultima as the general rules will permit.

 C. <u>Nouns</u> retain the accent on the same syllable on which it falls in the nominative singular form, insofar as the general rules permit.

 D. <u>Enclitics</u> are accented with the word preceding. For purposes of accenting, they count in general as additional syllables of the preceding word.

1. If an enclitic follows a word with an acute on the antepenult or a circumflex on the penult, the word preceding the enclitic takes an additional acute accent on the ultima.

2. If an enclitic of two syllables follows a word with an acute accent on the penult, the enclitic takes its own accent.

3. If an enclitic follows a proclitic or another enclitic, the first of the two takes an acute on the ultima.
   (<u>Exception</u>: οὐκ ἔστιν.)

4. If an enclitic follows a word with an accent on the ultima, no additional accent is necessary; but if the accent is acute, it of course does not become a grave.

5. An enclitic retains its own accent if it is to be emphasized or if it begins a clause.

6. When an enclitic retains its own accent, the accent is an acute on the ultima (which may become a grave).

V. Rules of vowel contraction. Ma 144-45; RD 34-35; Gr #3; DM 24-25

A. Two vowels which will form a diphthong do so.
   E.g., ε-ι form ει.

B. Two like vowels form their long.
   E.g., ε-η form η; α-α form long α.

   Exception: ε-ε form ει; ο-ο form ου.

C. An "o" vowel contracts with an "a" or an "e" vowel to form ω.
   E.g., α-o form ω.

   <u>Exceptions</u>: ε-ο or ο-ε form ου.

D. When an "a" vowel and an "e" vowel are contracted, the long of whichever is first is formed.
   E.g., ε-α form η ; α-η form long α.

E. When a vowel is contracted with a diphthong beginning with the same vowel, the first vowel disappears and the diphthong remains.
   E.g., o-ου form ου.

F. When a vowel is contracted with a diphthong beginning with a different vowel, the single vowel is contracted with the diphthong's first vowel according to the preceding rules.
   The diphthong's second vowel disappears if it is υ, or becomes a subscript if it is ι.
   E.g., α-ει form ᾳ.

   Exceptions: o-ει or o-η form οι.

VI. Movable ν. Gr #3h
   To facilitate pronunciation, the letter ν is added to datives plural ending in ι and to the third person of verbs ending in ε or ι (but not -ει) when they are followed by punctuation or by a vowel, and sometimes before δ and certain other consonants.

VII. Paradigms. Ma 225-51; Gr #9-117

A. Declension endings

   1. Key to all three declensions: the definite article and the indefinite pronoun. Gr #12-13; Ma 230, 236

   2. Classes of first declension nouns. Gr #17-20; Ma 225

      a. Vowel or ρ stem; nominative singular α
         (long or short)

Singular		Plural
Nom.	-α	-αι
Gen.	-ας	-ῶν
Dat.	-ᾳ	-αις
Acc.	-αν	-ας
Voc.	-α	-αι

b. Consonant stem; nominative singular α
   (long or short)

Nom.	-α	Plural:	same as <u>a</u>.
Gen.	-ης	above.	
Dat.	-ῃ		
Acc.	-αν		
Voc.	-α		

c. Nominative singular η

Nom.	-η	Plural:	same as <u>a</u>.
Gen.	-ης	above	
Dat.	-ῃ		
Acc.	-ην		
Voc.	-η		

d. Masculine nouns

Nom.	-ης	Plural:	same as <u>a</u>.
Gen.	-ου	above	
Dat.	-ῃ		
Acc.	-ην		
Voc.	-α		

3. Classes of second declension nouns.
   Gr #21-25; Ma 226

a. All except neuter nouns

	Singular	Plural
Nom.	-ος	-οι
Gen.	-ου	-ων
Dat.	-ῳ	-οις
Acc.	-ον	-ους
Voc.	-ε	-οι

b. Neuter nouns

	Singular	Plural
Nom.	-ον	-α
Gen.	-ου	-ων
Dat.	-ῳ	-οις
Acc.	-ον	-α
Voc.	-ον	-α

4. The third declension endings take various forms, due to contraction, etc. The stem must be learned from the genitive singular. The basic endings are as follows:

Singular		Plural
Nom. (various)		-ες
Gen.	-ος	-ων
Dat.	-ι	-σι
Acc.	-α	-ας
Voc. (various)		-ες

See also Gr #28-31; Ma 227-29.

B. Verb forms

1. Principal parts of verbs, and formation of regular verbs.

   a. Identification and formation
   First: Present active indicative first person singular.
   Verb stem plus ending -ω
   E.g., πιστεύω

   Second: Future active indicative first person singular.
   Verb stem plus σ tense suffix plus ending -ω
   E.g., πιστεύσω

   Third: Aorist active indicative first person singular.
   First aorist verbs, augmented verb stem plus σ tense suffix plus ending -α.
   E.g., ἐπίστευσα
   (Second aorist verbs are generally formed on augmented altered verb stem plus ending -ον.)

   Fourth: Perfect active indicative first person singular.
   Reduplicated verb stem plus ϰ tense suffix plus ending -α
   E.g., πεπίστευϰα

Fifth: Perfect middle (and passive)
indicative first person singular.
Reduplicated verb stem plus ending
- μαι (with no preceding variable
vowel)
E.g., πεπίστευμαι

Sixth: Aorist passive indicative first person
singular.
Augmented verb stem plus θ tense
suffix plus ending -ην
E.g., ἐπιστεύθην

b. Tenses derived from each principal part.
(All moods of a given tense are derived
from the same principal part)

First: Present active, middle and passive.
Imperfect active, middle and
passive (augment and secondary
ending)

Second: Future active and middle

Third: Aorist (first or second) active and
middle

Fourth: Perfect active
Pluperfect active (sometimes augment;
secondary ending)

Fifth: Perfect middle and passive
Pluperfect middle and passive
(sometimes augment; secondary
ending)

Sixth: Aorist passive
Future passive (remove augment;
add -ησ- plus primary ending).

2. Verb endings

a. The basic forms

<u>Primary</u> Active		<u>Primary</u> <u>Middle</u>	
–ω	–όμεν	–ομαι	–ομεθα
–εις	–ετε	–η	–εσθε
–ει	–ουσι	–εται	–ονται

<u>Secondary</u> Active		<u>Secondary</u> <u>Middle</u>	
–ον	–ομεν	–ομην	–ομεθα
–ες	–ετε	–ου	–εσθε
–ε	–ον	–ετο	–οντο

b. Use of the basic forms

    1) In tenses of the indicative mood, with modifications of the basic forms as required.

        a) · <u>Primary active endings</u>

            Present active

            Future active

        b) <u>Primary middle endings</u>

            Present middle and passive

            Future middle

            Future passive

            Perfect middle and passive: Omit the variable vowel. Second person singular, – σαι.

        c) <u>Secondary active endings</u>

            Imperfect active

            First aorist active: Variable vowel is α (ε in third person singular). (First person singular ending, – α.)

Second aorist active

Aorist passive: Variable vowel is η .
Third person plural ending, -ησαν.

Perfect active: Variable vowel is α
(ε in third person singular). (First
person singular ending, - α .)
Third person plural ending, - ασι.

Pluperfect active: Variable vowel
changes to ει . Third person plural
ending, -εισαν.

d) <u>Secondary</u> <u>middle</u> <u>endings</u>

Imperfect middle and passive

First aorist middle: Variable vowel
is α. Second person singular
ending, -ω.

Second aorist middle

Pluperfect middle and passive: No
variable vowel. Second person
singular ending, -σο.

2) The subjunctive mood. Ma 128-31

a) All tenses use primary endings (active
or middle, as indicative mood).

b) Variable vowel is lengthened: o becomes
ω, ε becomes η , ου becomes ω.

c) Stem augment is dropped from aorist.

d) Since the perfect middle and passive have
no variable vowel, these forms must be
written periphrastically in the subjunctive mood. (see 3, p. 11   below)

3) The imperative mood. Ma 177-80

a) Second person singular must be learned separately.

b) Second person plural in a given tense and voice is the same as the corresponding form of the <u>indicative</u> mood.

c) Third person singular is formed by substituting ω for the final ε of the second person plural of the same tense and voice.

d) Third person plural is formed by adding -σαν to the third person singular of the same tense and voice.

c. Infinitive endings

Present active: -ειν
Present middle and passive: -εσθαι

First aorist active: -αι
First aorist middle: -ασθαι
Second aorist active: -εῖν
Second aorist middle: -έσθαι
Aorist passive: -ῆναι

Perfect active: -έναι
Perfect middle and passive: -σθαι

d. Participial endings

1) All active participles and the aorist passive are declined like third, first, and third declension nouns.

Present active:
  Nom. sing. -ων, -ουσα, -ον
  Gen. sing. -οντος, -ουσης, -οντος

First aorist active:
  Nom. sing. -ας, -ασα, -αν
  Gen. sing. -αντος, ασης, -αντος

Second aorist active:
Nom. sing. -ών, -οῦσα, -όν
Gen. sing. -όντος, οὐσης, -όντος

Perfect active:
Nom. sing. -ώς, -υῖα, -ός
Gen. sing. -ότος, -υίας, -ότος

Aorist passive:
Nom. sing. -είς, -εῖσα, -έν
Gen. sing. -έντος, είσης, -έντος

2) All middle participles and all passives
except the aorist passive are declined
like second, first, and second declension
adjectives.

Present middle and passive:
-όμενος, -ομένη, -όμενον

First aorist middle:
-άμενος, -αμένη, -άμενον

Second aorist middle:
-όμενος, -ομένη, -όμενον

Perfect middle and passive:
-μένος, -μένη, -μένον

e. Learn to recognize forms of the -μι con-
jugation and of the optative mood.
Gr #104-17, 64, 74ff.; Ma 200-18, 244-51

3. Periphrastic tense formations. Bu 11, 16, 36, 40

Periphrastic forms may be translated like the
corresponding regular forms, but emphasize
either the progressive aspect or the resulting
state (see below).
E.g., compare ἔλυες and ἦς λύων

a. Tenses which use the present participle,

11

emphasizing the progressive aspect.

1) Present
   Present participle of a given verb,
   with the present tense of εἰμί.
   E.g., ἐστὶ λύων or λύων ἐστί.

2) Imperfect
   Present participle of a given verb,
   with the imperfect tense of εἰμί.
   E.g., ἦν λύων.

3) Future
   Present participle of a given verb,
   with the future tense of εἰμί.
   E.g., ἔσται λύων.

b. Tenses which use the perfect participle,
   possibly emphasizing the perfective aspect
   or the resulting state.

1) Perfect (present perfect)
   Perfect participle of a given verb,
   with the present tense of εἰμί.
   E.g., ἐστὶ λελυκώς or λελυκὼς ἐστι.

2) Pluperfect (past perfect)
   Perfect participle of a given verb,
   with the imperfect tense of εἰμί.
   E.g., ἦν λελυκώς.

3) Future perfect (this tense is always
   periphrastic in the New Testament)
   Perfect participle of a given verb,
   with the future tense of εἰμί.
   E.g., ἔσται λελυκώς.

c. In these periphrastic forms, all moods, in-
   cluding the infinitive, may be expressed
   by indicated modification.
   Mood is changed by changing mood of εἰμί.
   E.g., ὦ λύων.
   Voice is changed by changing voice of the

participle.

E.g., εἰμὶ λυόμενος.

Person and number are changed by making
the proper changes in εἰμί and the participle.

VIII. Adjectives

A. Attributive and predicate position. Ma 35-36, 54

1. When used with a noun which has the definite
   article, an adjective or participle in <u>attri-
   butive</u> position stands either between the noun
   and its article or following the noun with the
   article repeated before the adjective or participle. E.g., ὁ καλός λόγος or ὁ λόγος
   ὁ καλός

2. When used with a noun which has the definite
   article, an adjective or participle in <u>pre-
   dicate</u> position stands either before the
   noun and its article or following the noun
   without the repeated article. E.g., καλὸς
   ὁ λογὸς or ὁ λόγος καλός

3. When used with a noun which does <u>not</u> have the
   definite article, an adjective or participle
   may stand either before or following the noun,
   without an article, and may be either
   attributive or predicate position according to
   the requirements of the context.
   E.g., καλὸς λόγος or λόγος καλός

B. Types of adjectives. Gr #33-41; Ma 230-35

1. First and second declension adjectives
   The feminine gender is first declension. The
   vowel of the endings in the singular is <u>long</u> α
   if the stem ends in a vowel or ρ, otherwise η .
   E.g., ἀγαθός, ἀγαθή, ἀγαθόν.
   Participles of the middle voice (and all
   passives except the aorist) are declined thus.

13

A few adjectives are second declension only,
the feminine endings being identical with
the masculine. E.g., αἰώνιος, αἰώνιον.

2. First and third declension adjectives
The feminine gender is first declension.
The vowel of the feminine singular endings is
always short α. E.g.,πᾶς ,πᾶσα, πᾶν.
Participles of the active (and the aorist
passive) voice are declined thus, except
that the participles, following noun rule,
have a circumflex accent on the ultima of
the feminine genitive plural.

Some adjectives are third declension only,
the feminine endings being identical with
the masculine. E.g., ἀληθής, ἀληθές.

C. Comparison of adjectives. Gr #42-7; Ma 193

1. Comparative degree: stem plus -τερος,
-τέρα, τερον (first and second declensions).
Superlative degree: stem plus - τατος,
-τάτη, -τατον (first and second declensions).

E.g., ἰσχυρός, ἰσχυρότερος, ἰσχυρότατος

2. Comparative degree: stem (possibly modified)
plus - ίων, - ίων, - ίον (third declension).
Superlative degree: stem (possibly modified)
plus - ιστος, - ίστη, - ιστον (first and second
declensions).
E.g., μέγας, μείζων, μέγιστος.

3. Many adjectives have an irregular comparison.
E.g., ἀγαθός, κρείσσων, κράτιστος.

IX. Pronouns. Gr #53-62; Ma 235-37; MH 178-82

A. Personal

1. First person: "I," "we," etc.

Singular: ἐγώ, ἐμοῦ (μου), ἐμοί (μοι),
ἐμέ (με)
Plural: ἡμεῖς, ἡμῶν, ἡμῖν, ἡμᾶς.

2. Second person: "you," etc.
   Singular: σύ, σοῦ (σου), σοί (σοι),
   σέ (σε)
   Plural: ὑμεῖς, ὑμῶν; ὑμῖν, ὑμᾶς

3. Third person: "he," "she," "it," "they":
   αὐτός, declined like a first and second
   declension adjective, singular and plural.

B. Possessive: "my," "our," etc.
   The genitive case of the personal pronouns,
   commonly the unemphatic forms.

   (The possessive adjectives are first and second
   declension adjectives: First person singular
   ἐμός, plural ἡμέτερος; second person singular
   σός, plural ὑμέτερος. The emphatic
   possessive adjective, used with any person,
   is ἴδιος, -α, -ον, ("his own," etc.)

C. Intensive: "myself," "himself," etc., when used
   in apposition to a noun or pronoun.
   αὐτός in predicate position to its substantive
   antecedent.

D. Reflexive: "myself," "ourselves," etc., when
   used in the predicate to refer to an antecedent
   in the subject. (Not used in nominative.)

   1. First person singular: ἐμαυτοῦ etc.,
      first and second declension.

   2. Second person singular: σεαυτοῦ, etc.,
      first and second declension.

   3. Third person singular: ἑαυτοῦ, etc., first
      and second declension.

   4. Plural of all persons: ἑαυτῶν, etc., first
      and second declension.   15

The genitive case of the reflexive pronoun may
be used as an emphatic possessive pronoun
(Matt. 8:22).

E. Reciprocal: "one another"

Always plural, any gender, not used in nominative case.
ἀλλήλων, etc., first and second declension.

F. Relative: "who," "which"
ὅς, ἥ, ὅ, declined like a first and second declension adjective.

G. Interrogative: "who?" "which?"
τίς, τί declined according to the third declension. Acute accent on first syllable,
which is never changed to grave.

H. Indefinite: "someone," "something"
τις, τι, declined like the interrogative
pronoun, but enclitic.

I. Indefinite relative: "whoever," "whatever"
ὅστις, ἥτις, ὅτι. Used in nominative case
singular and plural, sometimes without indefinite force.

J. Demonstrative
"This": οὗτος, αὕτη, τοῦτο
"That": ἐκεῖνος, ἐκείνη, ἐκεῖνο
Declined like first and second declension
adjectives.

Greek letters are used as numerals, using a system more nearly resembling the Roman system than the Arabic, although differing from both. Because some letters were dropped from the Greek alphabet in very ancient times, three additional symbols are supplied as numerals: ⳤ (stigma), 6; ϙ (koppa), 90; and ϡ (sampi), 900. When letters are used as numerals an acute accent is placed over the final letter. An inverted acute accent placed under a letter multiplies that letter's numerical value by one thousand.

Symbol	Value	Name
ά	1	εἷς, μία, ἕν
β	2	δύο
γ	3	τρεῖς, τρία
δ	4	τέσσαρες, -α
ε	5	πέντε
ⳤ	6	ἕξ
ζ	7	ἑπτά
η	8	ὀκτώ
θ	9	ἐννέα
ι	10	δέκα
ιά	11	ἕνδεκα
ιβ	12	δώδεκα
ιγ	13	τρισκαίδεκα
ιδ	14	τεσσαρεσκαίδεκα
ιε	15	πεντεκαίδεκα
ιⳤ	16	ἑκκαίδεκα
κ	20	εἴκοσι(ν)
κά	21	εἴκοσι καὶ εἷς
κβ	22	εἴκοσι καὶ δύο
λ	30	τριάκοντα
μ	40	τεσσαράκοντα
ν	50	πεντήκοντα
ξ	60	ἑξήκοντα
ο	70	ἑβδομήκοντα
π	80	ὀγδοήκοντα
ϙ	90	ἐνενήκοντα
ρ	100	ἑκατόν
ς	200	διακόσιοι
τ	300	τριακόσιοι
υ	400	τετρακόσιοι
φ	500	πεντακόσιοι
χ	600	ἑξακόσιοι

Symbol	Value	Name
ψ	700	ἑπτακόσιοι
ω	800	ὀκτακόσιοι
ϡ	900	ἐνακόσιοι
͵α	1000	χίλιοι
͵αα	1001	χίλιοι καί εἷς
͵αρ	1100	χίλιοι καί ἑκατόν
͵β	2000	δισχίλιοι
͵δ	4000	τετρακισχίλιοι
͵ι	10000	μύριοι

εἷς is declined according to first and third declensions.

δύο is indeclinable except for the dative form δυσί(ν).

τρεῖς and τέσσαρες are declined according to the third declension.

The rest are indeclinable up to two hundred.

διακόσιοι (two hundred) and the remaining hundreds and thousands are declined according to the plural of the first and second declensions.

XI. Adverbs. Ma 194; Gr #126-34; Me 110

A. Principal correlative adverbs

Time	Demonstrative	Relative	Interrogative	Indefinite
	τότε, then	ὅτε,	πότε; when?	ποτε, some-
	νῦν, now	when		time
Place	ὧδε, here			
	αὐτοῦ, here,	οὗ,	ποῦ; where?	που, some-
	there	where		where
	ἐκεῖ, there			
	ἐντεῦθεν,	ὅθεν,	πόθεν; from	
	from here	from where	where?	
Manner	οὕτω(ς), thus, so	ὡς as	πῶς; how?	πως some-how

B. Corresponding to the English adverbial suffix "-ly," many Greek adverbs are formed by adding -ως to the stem of the corresponding adjective;
e.g., καλός, καλῶς.

C. Occasionally found is the adverbial suffix - θεν, "from."
   E. g.,ἐντεῦθεν, "from here," "hence."

XII. Word formation. Me 53-63; Gr #139-59

A. Suffixes

1. Principal suffixes forming nouns: signifying

Agent: - της (gen. - του)	Masc. 1st declen.
- ευς (gen. -έως)	Masc. 3rd declen.
Instrument: - τρον	Neut. 2nd declen.
Action or process: -σις (gen. -σεως)	Fem. 3rd declen.
-μος	Masc. 2nd declen.
Result, or the thing itself: - μα	
(gen. -ματος)	Neut. 3rd declen.
Quality: -ία or -οσύνη	Fem. 1st declen.
-της (gen. -ητος)	Fem. 3rd declen.
A diminutive: - ιον	Neut. 2nd declen.

a. Examples of the above, respectively:
   μαθητής, one who learns, a disciple
   βασιλεύς, one who rules, a king
   ἀμφιβλήστρον, an instrument for casting
                        around, a net
   κρίσις, the process of judging
   καθαρισμός, the process of cleansing
   γράμμα, the result of writing, a letter
   σοφία, the quality of being wise, wisdom
   δικαιοσύνη, the quality of being right-
                        eous, righteousness
   ἁγιότης, the quality of being holy,
                        holiness
   παιδίον, a small child

b. Exceptions
   The suffix of action is sometimes used
   to express result of action or the
   thing itself (cf. English "meeting" or
   "administration").
   E.g., κρίσις, used to express the action of judging, but sometimes the
   judgment handed down as a result
   (for κρίμα).

19

The diminutive suffix sometimes loses
its diminutive force. Other $-\iota o \nu$
nouns are not diminutives but substan-
tivized neuter forms of $-\iota o\varsigma$, $-\iota\alpha$,
$-\iota o \nu$ adjectives; e.g., $\beta\iota\beta\lambda\hat{\iota}o\nu$.

2. Principal suffixes forming adjectives: signifying

Quality: $-\eta\varsigma$, $-\varepsilon\varsigma$	3rd declension
Attribute or locality: $-\iota o\varsigma$, $(-\iota\alpha)$, $-\iota o\nu$	1st & 2nd decl. or 2nd only
Characteristics: $-\iota\kappa\acute{o}\varsigma$, $-\kappa\acute{\eta}$, $-\iota\kappa\acute{o}\nu$	1st & 2nd decl.
Material: $-\iota\nu o\varsigma$, $-\acute{\iota}\nu\eta$, $-\iota\nu o\nu$	1st & 2nd decl.
Fitness or ability: $-\iota\mu o\varsigma$, $-\iota\mu o\nu$	2nd declension
Possibility or actuality: $-\tau\acute{o}\varsigma$, $-\tau\acute{\eta}$, $-\tau\acute{o}\nu$	1st & 2nd decl.
Obligation or intention: $-\tau\acute{\varepsilon}o\varsigma$, $-\tau\acute{\varepsilon}\alpha$, $-\tau\acute{\varepsilon}o\nu$	1st & 2nd decl.

Examples of the above, respectively:

$\dot{\alpha}\lambda\eta\theta\acute{\eta}\varsigma$, $-\acute{\varepsilon}\varsigma$, the quality of being true

$\tau\acute{\iota}\mu\iota o\varsigma$, $-\alpha$, $-o\nu$, having the attribute of
honor, honorable

$o\dot{\upsilon}\rho\acute{\alpha}\nu\iota o\varsigma$, $-\alpha$, $-o\nu$, pertaining to heaven,
heavenly

$\beta\alpha\sigma\iota\lambda\iota\kappa\acute{o}\varsigma$, $-\acute{\eta}$, $-\acute{o}\nu$, having the character-
istics of a king, royal

$\lambda\acute{\iota}\theta\iota\nu o\varsigma$, $-\eta$, $-o\nu$, made of stone

$\chi\rho\acute{\eta}\sigma\iota\mu o\varsigma$, $-o\nu$, fit for use, useful

$\dot{\alpha}\pi\varepsilon\acute{\iota}\rho\alpha\sigma\tau o\varsigma$, $-\eta$, $-o\nu$, impossible to be
tempted, or untempted

$\beta\lambda\eta\tau\acute{\varepsilon}o\varsigma$, $-\alpha$, $-o\nu$, must be cast, or is to be cast

3. Principal suffixes forming verbs: signifying
(with exceptions) <u>To do</u> or <u>to be</u> what the
stem implies:

(E. g., $\dot{\alpha}\gamma\alpha\pi\acute{\alpha}\omega$, I love; $\dot{\varepsilon}\lambda\pi\acute{\iota}\zeta\omega$, I hope)
$-\acute{\alpha}\omega$, $-\acute{\varepsilon}\omega$, $-\varepsilon\acute{\upsilon}\omega$, $-\acute{\alpha}\zeta\omega$, $-\acute{\iota}\zeta\omega$

<u>To cause</u> what the stem implies:

(E.g.,$\theta\upsilon\mu\acute{o}\omega$, I cause to be angry; $\xi\eta\rho\alpha\acute{\iota}\nu\omega$,
I make dry) $-\acute{o}\omega$, $-\alpha\acute{\iota}\nu\omega$, $-\acute{\upsilon}\nu\omega$.

B. Prefixes. Gr #146-49; Me 102-09

    1. Prepositions. See meanings given for pre-
        positions in compound, pp. 33-47 below.

    2. Certain other particles: e.g., εὐ-, "well";
        ἀ -, "not"; δυσ-, "ill" or "mis-"

C. Nouns or verbs used to form compounds. Gr #148;
    Me 62
    E.g., καρδιογνώστης, one who knows the heart;
    θεόπνευστος, "God-breathed," inspired by
    God.

D. Examples of compounds and families of words.
    Gr #149; Me 65-94

    κρίνω, I judge
    κρίσις, the process of judging, judgment
    κρίμα, the result of judging, sentence
    κριτής, one who judges, a judge
    ἀνακρίνω, I examine
    ἀποκρίνομαι, I answer
    διακρίνω, I distinguish
    κατακρίνω, I condemn
    ὑποκρίτης, (one who is under a judge), an
                    actor, a hypocrite
    ἀδιάκριτος, not subject to distinction or hesi-
                    tation, impartial

SYNTAX

I. THE ARTICLE
Gr #193-234; RD 275-83; DM 137-53

A. General rule

1. Nouns <u>with</u> the definite article are generally
   either a) definite or b) generic. Jn. 1.1,
   ἐν ἀρχῇ ἦν ὁ λόγος, In the beginning
   was <u>the word</u>. 2.25, ἵνα τις μαρτυρήσῃ
   περὶ τοῦ ἀνθρώπου· αὐτὸς γὰρ ἐγίνωσκεν
   τί ἦν ἐν τῷ ἀνθρώπῳ, that anyone
   should testify concerning <u>man</u>; for he himself knew what was in man; (i.e., mankind).
   1.5, τὸ φῶς; 10.10, ὁ κλέπτης.

2. Nouns <u>without</u> the definite article are generally either a) indefinite or b) qualitative.
   Jn. 1.6, ἐγένετο ἄνθρωπος, There
   came <u>a man</u>. 1.4, ἐν αὐτῷ ζωὴ ἦν,
   In him was life. 1.12, τέκνα;
   σάρξ.

B. Applications of the general rule

1. A word in <u>predicate</u> position is changed to
   attributive position by the article; e.g.,
   ὁ λόγος καλός, "The word is good,"
   is thus changed to ὁ λόγος ὁ καλός,
   "the good word."

2. A word which is indefinite is changed to
   definite by the article; e.g., ἄνθρωπος,
   "a man," is thus changed to ὁ ἄνθρωπος, "the man."

3. A separate article preceding various words
   and phrases implies an understood noun
   which agrees with the article, and thus
   makes a substantive expression of the word
   or phrase.

   a. With an adverb. ἐπαύριον, "next,
      following"; ἡ ἐπαύριον (ἡμέρα
      understood), "the following day, to-
      morrow." πλησίον, "next, adjacent";
      ὁ πλησίον (ἄνθρωπος understood),
      "the adjacent person, neighbor."

   b. With a genitive word or phrase. τοῦ
      Ἰωάννου, "of John"; οἱ τοῦ Ἰωάννου,
      "the servants (sons, disciples, etc.) of
      John."

   c. With clauses, quotations, etc. εἰ δύνῃ,
      "If you are able"; τὸ εἰ δύνῃ, "The 'if
      you are able' statement" (cf. Mk. 9.22-23).
      τὸ τί ἂν θέλοι καλεῖσθαι αὐτό,
      "The what-he-might-wish-him-to-be-
      called question," Lk. 1.62.

4. With the copulative verbs εἰμί and
   γίνομαι, which take the nominative case
   in predicate as well as subject, a noun with
   the article is normally the subject and a noun
   without the article is normally the predicate.
   Jn. 18.40, ἦν δὲ ὁ Βαραββᾶς λῃστής,
   Now Barabbas was a robber, 8.42, εἰ
   ὁ θεὸς πατὴρ ὑμῶν ἦν.
   But if the predicate is definite or is identical
   with the subject it will have an article also.
   Jn. 1.4, ἡ ζωὴ ἦν τὸ φῶς, the life was the

light. 6.33, ὁ γὰρ ἄρτος...ἐστιν ὁ
καταβαίνων.
Of course, if the subject is indefinite or qualitative it will not have an article. 1.4, ἐν
αὐτῷ ζωὴ ἦν, In him was life. 4.46,
καὶ ἦν τις βασιλικός.

However, when a predicate noun <u>precedes</u>
the copulative verb it normally does <u>not</u>
have an article regardless of whether it is
definite or indefinite. Jn. 9.5, φῶς εἰμι
τοῦ κόσμου (cf. 8.12), I am the light of the
world. 10.36, υἱὸς τοῦ θεοῦ εἰμι.
Mk. 15.39, υἱὸς θεοῦ ἦν.

4.   The article is used with monadic nouns (ob-
jects of which there is but one); e.g.,
"heaven," "earth," etc. (Sometimes they
follow the rule governing proper nouns.)
Jn. 3.31, ἐκ τῆς γῆς, of the only earth there
is. 3.31, ἐκ τοῦ οὐρανοῦ.

5.   The article is used with nouns which are <u>set</u>
<u>apart</u> and distinguished from their class.
Jn. 3.14, ἐν τῇ ἐρήμῳ, in <u>the</u> desert, (the
particular desert in the area where the
event occurred). Jn. 5.39, τὰς γραφάς,
the Scriptures (the general term γραφαί,
"writings," used here to designate a
special group of writings, viz. the Scriptures). Mt. 12.41, τῇ κρίσει.

6.   The article is used, in the <u>generic</u> sense,
with nouns <u>typical</u> of their class, in prov-
erbs, general truths, etc. Lk. 10.7,
ἄξιος γὰρ ὁ ἐργάτης τοῦ μισθοῦ αὐτοῦ,
for <u>the</u> workman (any workman) is worthy
of his wages. Jn. 10.10, ὁ κλέπτης.

7.   The article is used for renewed mention of
a noun, even if it had no article in its first
occurrence. Jn. 4.43, μετὰ δὲ τὰς δύο
ἡμέρας, And after <u>the</u> two days (the days
referred to as "two days" in 4.40). Jn.
2.9, τὸ ὕδωρ (cf. 2.7).

8. The article is used with abstract nouns objec-
tified or personified. Jn. 1.17, ἡ χάρις καὶ
ἡ ἀλήθεια . . .ἐγένετο, grace and
truth came (contrast χάριν ἀντὶ χάριτος
immediately preceding). Acts 28.4, ἡ δίκη.

9. When possession is obvious, the possessive
pronoun is sometimes omitted and the article, by making the noun definite, implies
the possession also. Jn. 7.30, οὐδεὶς
ἐπέβαλεν ἐπ' αὐτὸν τὴν χεῖρα , no one
put the hand (i.e., his hand) upon him. Jn. 3.17,
τὸν υἱόν.

10. When a demonstrative pronoun is used with
a noun, the noun must have the article and
the demonstrative pronoun must stand in
predicate position. Jn. 7.36,τίς ἐστιν ὁ
λόγος οὗτος; What is this word?
When there is no article, the demonstrative
must be considered as standing alone. Jn. 6.42,
οὐχ οὗτός ἐστιν 'Ιησοῦς ὁ υἱὸς 'Ιωσήφ;
Is not this man Jesus the son of Joseph?
("This" is the subject, "Jesus" is the predicate.)

11. When the nominative case is used for the
vocative, the noun takes the article. Jn.
19.3, χαίρε ὁ βασιλεὺς τῶν 'Ιουδαίων.
Hail, King of the Jews! Jn. 20.28,
ὁ κύριος . . . ὁ θεός.

12. "Granville Sharp's rule": When the article is
used before only the first member of a
series, the members are to be considered
as a connected whole. When the article is
used before each member, each is to be
considered separately. Eph. 3.18,τὸ πλάτος
καὶ μῆκος καὶ ὕψος καὶ βάθος ,
the width and length and height and depth
(as one image). Lk. 12.11, ἐπὶ τὰς
συναγωγὰς καὶ τὰς ἀρχὰς καὶ τὰς
ἐξουσίας , to the synagogues and the rulers
and the authorities (considered separately).
Jn. 7.45, τοὺς ἀρχιερεῖς καὶ Φαρισαίους.
Heb. 11.20, τὸν 'Ιακὼβ καὶ τὸν Ἡσαῦ.

C. Exceptions to the general rule

1. In some idiomatic or set phrases, a defining
   or qualifying word or phrase may make a
   noun definite even though the noun has no article. (These instances are limited to those in
   which the noun clearly must be considered
   definite in the context.) The defining phrase
   is usually also anarthrous. Jn. 12.13, ἐν ὀνο-
   ματι κυρίου, in the name of the Lord
   (obviously, not "in a name . . ."). Acts
   11.21, χεὶρ κυρίου.

2. In some prepositional phrases which are
   idioms of time, place, etc., the object
   of the preposition has no article but is
   nevertheless definite (cf. the English phrases
   "at home," "on land," etc.). Jn. 1.1,2,
   ἐν ἀρχῇ, in the beginning. Lk. 15.25,
   ἐν ἀγρῷ.

3. Nouns written in the vocative case are definite, but have no article. Jn. 4.15,
   κύριε, δός μοι τοῦτο τὸ ὕδωρ,
   Sir, give me this water. Jn. 2.4, γύναι.

4. (Partial exception to general rule) Proper
   names of persons and places, and divine names
   and titles, are definite in themselves; they
   may or may not take the article. Jn. 1.43-44,
   τὴν Γαλιλαίαν . . . Φίλιππον . . .
   ὁ Ἰησοῦς . . . ὁ Φίλιππον . . . Βηθσαι-
   δά, Galilee . . . Philip . . . Jesus . . .
   Philip . . . Bethsaida. Jn. 3.2, ἀπὸ θεοῦ
   ἐλήλυθας, you have come from God.
   3.2, ἐὰν μὴ ᾖ ὁ θεὸς μετ' αὐτοῦ,
   unless God be with him. Jn. 2.1, Κανὰ τῆς
   Γαλιλαίας . . . τοῦ Ἰησοῦ.
   At the same time, when a divine title ("God," "Holy
   Spirit") has the article there may be emphasis
   upon the person--i.e., who he is; and when a divine
   title has no article there may be emphasis upon the

<u>nature</u> or activity--i.e., <u>what</u> he is. Jn. 1.1,
ὁ λόγος ἦν πρὸς τὸν θεόν, καὶ θεὸς ἦν
ὁ λόγος , the Word was with God (the
Father considered as a person), and the
Word was Deity (not identical with God the
Father, but of the nature or quality of God).
II Cor. 4.4, ὁ θεὸς τοῦ αἰῶνος τούτου,
the god of this age (a definite "god," but
not God).

D. With μέν or δέ, the article is actually a pronoun
in usage, conveying slight emphasis. In narra-
tion, ὁ δέ calls attention to a change of person
referred to. Jn. 7.12, οἱ μὲν ἔλεγον, <u>some</u>
were saying, Jn. 4.31-32, ἡρώτων αυτὸν οἱ
μαθηταὶ . . . ὁ δὲ εἶπεν , the disciples were
asking him . . . but <u>he</u> said. Acts 14.4, οἱ μὲν
. . οἱ δέ. Jn. 5.17, ὁ δὲ ἀπεκρίνατο.

II. USE OF CASES
   (Exclusive of cases after prepositions)
          Gr #241-87

A. <u>Nominative</u> <u>and</u> <u>vocative</u>

   1. Nominative: subject of finite verb. Jn. 1.4, ἡ ζωὴ
       ἦν τὸ φῶς τῶν ἀνθρώπων, <u>the life</u>
       was the light of men. 1.2, οὗτος.

   2. Nominative: predicate of copulative verb.
       Jn. 1.4, ἡ ζωὴ ἦν τὸ φῶς τῶν ἀνθρώπων,
       the life was <u>the light</u> of men. 1.8, τὸ φῶς.

   3. Nominative: sometimes used for the voca-
       tive (see <u>I.B.11</u> above). Jn. 19.3, χαῖρε ὁ
       βασιλεὺς τῶν Ἰουδαίων, Hail, <u>King</u> of
       the Jews! 20.28, ὁ κύριος μου καὶ ὁ θεός
       μου.

   4. Vocative: used in direct address, with or
       without the interjection ὦ. Jn. 19.26, γύναι,
       ἴδε , Woman, behold. Acts 1.1, Τὸν μὲν
       πρῶτον λόγον ἐποιησάμην . . . , ὦ

Θεόφιλε,   The former treatise I made
. . ., O Theophilus. Jn. 4.15, κύριε.

B.   Genitive

1.   Possession. Jn. 1.12, τέκνα θεοῦ, children
who belong to God. 1.29, τοῦ κόσμου.

2.   Source or author. Rom. 4.13, διὰ δικαιοσύνης
πίστεως , through (the righteous-
ness of faith (i.e., which has its
source in faith). Rom. 15.4, τῶν γραφῶν.

3.   Subjective. Modifying a noun of action, this
genitive expresses the doer of that action.
Jn. 2.6, λίθιναι ὑδρίαι ἓξ κατὰ τὸν
καθαρισμὸν τῶν Ἰουδαίων , six stone
water jars for the cleansing-rites of the Jews
(i.e., which the Jews performed). Acts 1.22,
Ἰωάννου.

4.   Objective. Modifying a noun of action, this
genitive expresses the receiver of that action. (Contrast the subjective genitive.)
Jn. 3.1, ἄρχων τῶν Ἰουδαίων, a ruler of
the Jews (i.e., one who ruled over the
Jews). 3.10, ὁ διδάσκαλος τοῦ Ἰσραήλ.

5.   Material. Mk. 2.21, ἐπίβλημα ῥάκους
ἀγνάφου, a patch (made) of unshrunk cloth.

6.   Contents. Jn. 2.7, γεμίσατε τὰς ὑδρίας
ὕδατος , Fill the water-jars with water.
4.14, πηγὴ ὕδατος.

7.   Partitive. Modifies another noun, this genitive expressing the whole of that of which
the other noun expresses part. Jn. 2.11, ἀρχὴν
τῶν σημείων , the beginning of the
miracle-signs. 2.11, ἐν Κανὰ τῆς
Γαλιλαίας, in Cana (which is a part) of
Galilee. 4.39, πολλοὶ . . . τῶν Σαμαριτῶν.

8. Apposition. (Cf. English "the city of Chicago.") Eph. 6.14, τὸν θώρακα τῆς δικαιοσύνης, the breastplate which is righteousness. Eph. 6.16, τὸν θυρεὸν τῆς πίστεως . Eph. 6.17, τὴν περικεφαλαίαν τοῦ σωτηρίου.

   (Apposition is more commonly expressed by using the same case as that of the noun with which apposition is intended, as in English. Jn. 1.23, 'Ησαῖας ὁ προφήτης, Isaiah the prophet.)

9. Comparison. The first member of the comparison takes its normal case; the second member is in the genitive case. Jn. 4.12, μὴ σὺ μείζων εἶ τοῦ πατρὸς ·ἡμῶν 'Ιακώβ; Are you greater than our father Jacob? 13.16, δοῦλος μείζων τοῦ κυρίου. . . ἀπόστολος μείζων τοῦ πέμψαντος αὐτόν. 21.15, ἀγαπᾷς με πλέον τούτων; (But comparison may also be expressed by using ἤ, "than," with both members in the case required by the first member. Jn. 3.19, ἠγάπησαν οἱ ἄνθρωποι μᾶλλον τὸ σκότος ἢ τὸ φῶς , men loved the darkness rather than the light.)

10. Price, equivalent, or penalty. Jn. 12.5, διὰ τί τοῦτο τὸ μύρον οὐκ ἐπράθη τριακοσίων δηναρίων; Why was this ointment not sold for the price of 300 denarii? Mt. 10.29, ἀσσαρίου.

11. Time or place within which. Jn. 3.2, οὗτος ἦλθεν πρὸς αὐτὸν νυκτός , This man came to him during the night. Lk. 18.7, ἡμέρας καὶ νυκτός

12. Quality. Includes abstract nouns used with adjectival force. Gal. 6.1. ἐν πνεύματι πραΰτητος, in a spirit of gentleness (i.e., a gentle spirit). Rom. 1.26, εἰς πάθη

ἀτιμίας. I Pet. 1.14, τέκνα ὑπακοῆς.

13. Predicate of various verbs, and with related adjectives:

    a. Sense perceptions, memory, etc. Jn. 15.20, μνημονεύετε τοῦ λόγου, Remember the word. 20.17, μή μου ἅπτου. ἀκούω normally takes the accusative of the <u>thing</u> heard and the genitive of the <u>person</u> heard. Jn. 3.8, τὴν φωνὴν αὐτοῦ ἀκούεις , you hear its sound. 1.37, ἤκουσαν οἱ δύο μαθηταὶ αὐτοῦ λαλοῦντος, the two disciples heard <u>him</u> speaking.

    b. Partaking, attaining (a part of). Jn. 8. 52, οὐ μὴ γεύσηται θανάτου, he will by no means taste (of) death. Lk. 20.35, τοῦ αἰῶνος ἐκείνου τυχεῖν.

    c. Fullness, lack, etc. Jn. 1.14, πλήρης χάριτος καὶ ἀληθείας, full of grace and truth. Rom. 3.23, πάντες. . . ὑστεροῦνται τῆς δόξης τοῦ θεοῦ.

    d. Accusing, etc. Jn. 5.45, μὴ δοκεῖτε ὅτι ἐγὼ κατηγορήσω ὑμῶν, Do not think that I will accuse <u>you</u>. Acts 19.40, ἐγκαλεῖσθαι στάσεως.

    e. Separation. Acts 27.43, ἐκώλυσεν αὐτοὺς τοῦ βουλήματος , he restrained them <u>from the plan</u>. Eph. 2.12, ἀπηλλοτριωμένοι τῆς πολιτείας.

14. General relationship. After various nouns and adjectives, a genitive not easily definable except in general terms or in terms suggested by each context. Jn. 5.29, ἀνάστασιν ζωῆς . . . ἀνάστασιν κρίσεως, a resurrection leading to life . . . a resurrection leading to judgment. 7.35, τὴν

διασπορὰν τῶν Ἑλλήνων.

15. Genitive absolute. A noun or pronoun with a
    participle, independent of the rest of the
    clause. Jn. 2.3, καὶ ὑστερήσαντος οἴνου,
    And when the wine failed. 5.13, ὄχλου ὄντος.

C. **Dative**

1. Indirect object of a verb. Jn. 1.25, εἶπαν
   αὐτῷ, they said to him. 1.26, ἀπεκρίθη
   αὐτοῖς. (But sometimes an indirect object is expressed by πρός and the accusative case. Jn. 2.3, λέγει ἡ μήτηρ τοῦ
   Ἰησοῦ πρὸς αὐτόν, the mother of Jesus said
   to him.)

2. Possession, in predicate of a copulative verb.
   Jn. 13.35, ἐμοὶ μαθηταί ἐστε, you are disciples to me (i.e., my disciples). Mt. 18.12,
   ἐὰν γένηταί τινι ἀνθρώπῳ.

3. Predicate of various verbs, and with related
   adjectives, expressing association, simi-
   larity, fitness, etc. Jn. 5.10, οὐκ ἔξεστίν
   σοι, it is not lawful _for you_. 9.9, ὅμοιος αὐτῷ
   ἐστιν.

4. Instrument or means. Jn. 11.2, ἦν δὲ Μαριὰμ ἡ
   ἀλείψασα τὸν κύριον μύρῳ καὶ ἐκμάξασα
   τοὺς πόδας αὐτοῦ ταῖς θριξὶν αὐτῆς,
   Now it was Mary who had anointed
   the Lord with _ointment_ and wiped his feet
   with her _hair_. 11.44, χειρίαις... σουδαρίῳ.
   (Occasionally used instead of ὑπό with
   the genitive to express personal agent.
   Lk. 23.15, οὐδὲν ἄξιον θανάτου ἐστίν
   πεπραγμένον αὐτῷ , nothing worthy of
   death has been done _by him_. "To him," as
   indirect object, would obviously be wrong.)

5. Cause or motive. Rom. 4.20, οὐ διεκρίθη τῇ

31

ἀπιστίᾳ , he did not hesitate <u>because of</u> unbelief. Gal. 6.12, τῷ σταυρῷ.

6. Time when. Jn. 2.1, τῇ ἡμέρᾳ τῇ τρίτῃ, on the third day. 6.54, τῇ ἐσχάτῃ ἡμέρᾳ.

7. Reference. The sphere, or the thing with regard to which something is done. Jn.3. 26, ᾧ σὺ μεμαρτύρηκας, he <u>with reference to whom</u> you have testified. Mt. 5.3, τῷ πνεύματι.

8. Measure or degree. Jn. 4.41, πολλῷ πλείους ἐπίστευσαν , more people <u>by much</u> believed (i.e., many more people).

9. Manner or mode. Phil 1. 18, παντὶ τρόπῳ, εἴτε προφάσει εἴτε ἀληθείᾳ, Χριστὸς καταγγέλλεται , <u>in every manner,</u> whether <u>in pretence</u> or <u>in truth,</u> Christ is being proclaimed. Acts 15. 1, τῷ ἔθει.

10. May repeat the idea of the verb. Jn. 3.29, χαρᾷ χαίρει , he rejoices <u>with joy</u> (i.e., he rejoices greatly). Lk. 22.15, ἐπιθυμίᾳ ἐπεθύμησα.

D. <u>Accusative</u>

1. Direct object of a verb. Jn. 3.16, ἠγάπησεν ὁ θεὸς τὸν κόσμον, God loved the world. 3.17, τὸν υἱόν.

2. Subject of an infinitive. Jn. 3.14, ὑψωθῆναι δεῖ τὸν υἱὸν τοῦ ἀνθρώπου , it is necessary for <u>the Son</u> of Man to be lifted up. 2.24, διὰ τὸ αὐτὸν γινώσκειν πάντας , because of <u>his</u> knowing all people. 21.22, ἐὰν αὐτὸν θέλω μένειν . 1.48, πρὸ τοῦ σε Φίλιππον φωνῆσαι .

3. Extent of time or space. Jn. 1.39, ἔμειναν τὴν ἡμέραν ἐκείνην , they remained (during) that day. 6.19 ἐληλακότες οὖν ὡς

σταδίους εἴκοσι πέντε ἤ τριάκοντα,

Then when they had rowed about 25 or 30
stadia. 2.12, οὐ πολλὰς ἡμέρας.

4. Cognate accusative. Extends or emphasizes
the meaning of a verb by a word related in
meaning. (Cf. dative of mode.) Jn. 7.24,
τὴν δικαίαν κρίσιν κρίνατε , judge
righteous judgment (i.e., judge righteously).
Mt. 2.10, χαρὰν μεγάλην.

III. PREPOSITIONS
Gr #118-25, 234-307; DM 113

A. Principal uses and meanings

1. ἀμφί (not used as a separate preposition in
the New Testament)

In compound: Round about. Mt. 4.18,
βάλλοντας ἀμφιβλῆστρον , casting a net--
literally, an instrument (-τρον) for casting
(-βλη-, from βάλλω) around (ἀμφι-). Mk.
11.4, ἀμφόδου.

2. ἀνά (general meaning up, opposite of κατά)

With the accusative:
a. Throughout. Mk. 7.31, ἀνὰ μέσον τῶν
ὀρίων Δεκαπόλεως , throughout the
midst of the regions of Decapolis.
Mt. 13.25, ἀνὰ μέσον τοῦ σίτου.
b. Apiece (distributive). Jn. 2.6, χωροῦσαι
ἀνὰ μετρητὰς δύο ἤ τρεῖς ,
holding two or three measures apiece.
Mt. 20.9, ἔλαβον ἀνὰ δηνάριον.

In compound:
a. Up. Jn. 1.51,ἀναβαίνοντας, ascend-
ing (going up). Jn. 5.29, ἀνάστασιν.
b. Back again. Lk. 15.24, ἀνέζησεν, he
has come to life again. Col. 3.10, τὸν
ἀνακαινούμενον .

c. Intensive use. Lk. 23.18, ἀνέκραγον
they were crying out. Lk. 12.49, ἀνήφθη.

3. ἀντί (general meaning in place of)

With the genitive:
  a. In place of, instead of. Mt. 2.22, ἀντί
     του πατρὸς αὐτου , in place of
     his father. Lk. 11.11, ἀντί ἰχθύος.
  b. In exchange for. Mt. 5.38, ὀφθαλμὸν ἀντί
     ὀφθαλμοῦ , eye for an eye. Heb.
     12.16, ἀντί βρώσεως μιᾶς.
  c. Cause, for. Eph. 5.31. ἀντί τούτου,
     because of this. Heb. 12.2, ἀντί της
     προκειμένης αὐτῷ χαρᾶς. (Al-
     ternative meaning here, instead of.)
  d. In behalf of, for. Mt. 17.27, δὸς αὐτοῖς
     ἀντί ἐμοῦ καὶ σοῦ , give it to
     them for (in behalf of) me and you.
     Mt. 20.28, ἀντί πολλῶν.

In compound:
  a. Opposite to. Jn. 19.12, πᾶς ὁ βασιλέα
     ἑαυτὸν ποιῶν ἀντιλέγει τῷ Καίσαρι,
     Everyone who makes himself a king
     speaks against Caesar. I Jn. 2.18,

     ἀντίχριστος.

  b. In return. Lk. 6.38, ᾧ γὰρ μέτρῳ
     μετρεῖτε ἀντιμετρηθήσεται ὑμῖν
     For with the measure with which you
     measure it shall be measured back to
     you in return. Ro. 1.27, ἀντιμισθίαν.

4. ἀπό (general meaning away from the exterior,
   opposite of πρός)

With the genitive:
  a. Away from (separation). Jn. 10.18, οὐδεὶς
     ἦρεν αὐτὴν ἀπ' ἐμοῦ , No one
     takes it away from me. Jn. 10.5, ἀπ'
     αὐτοῦ.

  b. From (source, derivation). Jn. 3.2, οἴδαμεν

34

ὅτι ἀπὸ θεοῦ ἐλήλυθας , we
know that you have come from God.
Jn. 1.45, ἀπὸ Ναζαρέθ.

In compound:
a. Away from (separation). Jn. 12.42, ἵνα μὴ
   ἀποσυνάγωγοι γένωνται , lest
   they should become excommunicated
   (separated from the synagogue). Lk.
   23.14, ἀποστρέφοντα.
b. Completely (intensive). Lk. 6.10,
   ἀπεχατεστάθη ἡ χεὶρ αὐτοῦ,
   his hand was completely restored.
   Mk. 13.22, ἀποπλανᾶν.

5. διά

With the genitive: Through.
a. Through (of place). Jn. 4.4, διὰ τῆς
   Σαμαρείας, through Samaria. Jn. 10.1,
   διὰ τῆς θύρας.
b. Through (of time). Mk. 14.58, διὰ τριῶν
   ἡμέρων , through three days.
   Lk. 5.5, δι ὅλης νυκτός.
c. Through (of agency). Jn. 1.3, δι' αὐτοῦ,
   through him. Jn. 1.17, διὰ Μωϋσέως.

With the accusative:
On account of. Jn. 1.31, διὰ τοῦτο, on
   account of this. Jn. 3.29, διὰ τὴν φωνήν.

In compound:
a. Through. Jn. 4.4, διέρχεσθαι, to go
   through. Lk. 16.26, διαβῆναι.
b. Thoroughly (intensive). Ac. 8.1, πάντες
   δὲ διεσπάρησαν , and all were
   scattered about. Lk. 2.51, διετήρει.

6. εἰς (general meaning into the interior, opposite of ἐκ)

With the accusative:
a. Into a place, state, or time. Jn. 1.9,
   ἐρχόμενον εἰς τὸν κόσμον, coming
   into the world. Jn. 1.43, εἰς τὴν Γαλιλαίαν. Jn. 6.51, εἰς τὸν αἰῶνα.

b. Regarding, against. Jn. 8.26, ταῦτα
λαλῶ εἰς τὸν κόσμον, these
things I speak with regard to the world.
Jn. 15.21, εἰς ὑμᾶς.

c. Purpose. Jn. 9.39, εἰς κρίμα, for
the purpose of judgment. Jn. 1.7,
εἰς μαρτυρίαν.

d. Result (as distinct from purpose).
Heb. 11.3, πίστει νοοῦμεν κατηρτί-
σθαι τοὺς αἰῶνας ῥήματι θεοῦ, εἰς
τὸ μὴ ἐκ φαινομένων τὸ βλεπόμενον
γεγονέναι, By faith we understand
that the worlds were formed by the
word of God, with the result that that
which is seen has not been made from
things which appear. Ro. 1.20, εἰς
τὸ εἶναι αὐτοὺς ἀναπολογήτους.

e. Equivalence (substantive or noun expression).
Jn. 16.20, ἡ λύπη ὑμῶν εἰς χαρὰν
γενήσεται, your grief shall become
joy. Heb. 1.5, εἰς πατέρα . . .
εἰς υἱόν.

f. In (generally with verbs of state, meaning
to be in as a result of having previously
gone into. Cf. the similar "pregnant
construction" of ἐν.) Jn. 1.18, ὁ
ὢν εἰς τὸν κόλπον τοῦ πατρός,
who has gone into the bosom of the Father
and is now in his bosom. Mk 10.10, εἰς
τὴν οἰκίαν . . . ἐπηρώτων αὐτόν.

Note: The idea of the regular N. T. usage of
εἰς and the accusative with πιστεύω
is to put one's faith into someone or
something. It is therefore a completely
regular example of a. above, not f,
even though the usual English idiom
for translating it is to "believe in" or

36

"on." Jn. 2.11, ἐπίστευσαν εἰς
αὐτὸν οἱ μαθηταὶ αὐτοῦ.

In compound:

> Into. Jn. 10.9, δι’ ἐμοῦ ἐάν τις
> εἰσέλθῃ, If anyone enters through me.
> Jn. 18.16, εἰσήγαγεν.

7. ἐκ (general meaning <u>from</u> the <u>interior</u> to the
    <u>exterior</u>, opposite of εἰς)

With the genitive:

a. Out of (place). Jn. 2.15, πάντας ἐξ-
    έβαλεν ἐκ τοῦ ἱεροῦ,   he drove
    them all out of the temple. Jn. 7.38,
    ἐκ τῆς κοιλίας αὐτοῦ.

b. <u>From</u> (source). Jn. 3.27, ἐὰν μὴ ἦ
    δεδομένον αὐτῷ ἐκ τοῦ οὐρανοῦ,
    unless it be given to him from heaven.
    Jn. 1.13, οὐκ ἐξ αἱμάτων οὐδὲ ἐκ
    θελήματος σαρκὸς οὐδὲ ἐκ θελή-
    ματος ἀνδρὸς ἀλλ’ ἐκ θεοῦ.

c. For, from (time). Jn. 9.32, ἐκ τοῦ αἰῶ-
    νος οὐκ ἠκούσθη, From eternity it has
    not been heard. Jn. 9.24, ἐκ δευτέρου.

d. <u>From</u> (cause). Jn. 4.6, κεκοπιακὼς ἐκ
    τῆς ὁδοιπορίας, wearied from
    (because of) his journey.

e. <u>Out of</u> (material). Jn. 2.15, ποιήσας
    φραγέλλιον ἐκ σχοινίων, having made
    a whip out of cords. Jn. 19.2, ἐξ ἀκανθῶν.

f. <u>Of</u> (partitive). Jn. 1.35, ὁ Ἰωάννης καὶ ἐκ
    τῶν μαθητῶν αὐτοῦ δύο, John and two
    (who were a part) of his disciples. Jn. 6.60,
    πολλοὶ . . . ἐκ τῶν μαθητῶν αὐτοῦ.

In compound:

a. <u>Forth</u>, out. Jn. 2.15, πάντας ἐξέβαλεν,
    he drove them all out. Jn. 5.29, ἐκπορεύ-
    σονται.

b. <u>Completely</u> (perfective). Lk. 21.36, δεό-
    μενοι ἵνα κατισχύσητε ἐκφυγεῖν,

37

praying that you may have strength to
escape (to flee successfully). Lk. 14.
30, ἐκτελέσαι.

8. ἐν (general meaning in)

With the dative:
a. In (place or state). Jn. 1.4, ἐν αὐτῷ,
   in him. Jn. 1.10, ἐν τῷ κόσμῳ.
b. Among. Jn. 1.14, ἐσκήνωσεν ἐν ἡμῖν,
   dwelt among us. Jn. 9.16, ἐν αὐτοῖς.
c. At, when, (with a point of time). Lk. 2.27,
   ἐν τῷ εἰσαγαγεῖν τοὺς γονεῖς τὸ
   παιδίον , when the parents brought
   in the child (i.e., at their bringing
   him in). Jn. 2.23, ἐν τῇ ἑορτῇ.
d. With, by (instrumental). Jn. 1.33, οὗτός
   ἐστιν ὁ βαπτίζων ἐν πνεύματι
   ἁγίῳ, this is he who baptizes with the
   Holy Spirit. Lk. 11.20, ἐν δακτύλῳ
   θεου.
e. In the power of. Jn. 3.21, ὅτι ἐν θεῷ εἰρ-
   γασμένα, that they have been
   wrought in the power of God. Jn. 5.43,
   ἐν τῷ ὀνόματι.
f. Invested with. I Ti. 1.18, ἵνα στρατεύῃ
   ἐν αὐταῖς , in order that you
   may fight invested with them. Heb.
   9.25, ἐν αἵματι ἀλλοτρίῳ.
g. In (the phrase being the equivalent of an
   adverb). Jn. 7.4, ἐν κρυπτῷ ... ἐν
   παρρησίᾳ, in secret (i.e., secretly)
   ... in the open (i.e., openly). Jn.
   7.10, ἐν κρυπτῷ.
h. Into (with verbs of action, meaning a
   motion into resulting in now being in.
   Cf. the similar "pregnant construction" of εἰς.) Lk. 23.19, ὅστις ἦν . . .
   βληθεὶς ἐν τῇ φυλακῇ, who had
   been cast into prison and was now in
   prison. Jn. 3.35, δέδωκεν ἐν τῇ χειρὶ
   αὐτοῦ.

In compound:

    In, into, at. Rom. 4.20, ἐνεδυναμώθη τῇ πίστει, he was enabled by faith. Jn. 6.17, ἐμβάντες εἰς πλοῖον.

9. ἐπί (general meaning upon)

With the genitive:

    a. Upon. Jn. 6.2, ἐπὶ τῶν ἀσθενούντων, upon the sick. Jn. 6.19, ἐπὶ τῆς θαλάσσης.

    b. At the time of. Lk. 4.27, ἐπὶ Ἐλισαίου τοῦ προφήτου, at the time of Elisha the prophet. Lk. 3.2, ἐπὶ ἀρχιερέως Αννα καὶ Καιφᾶ.

With the dative:

    At, upon (place, basis). Mk. 1.22, ἐξεπλήσσοντο ἐπὶ τῇ διδαχῇ αὐτοῦ, they were astonished at his teaching. Jn. 4.6, ἐπὶ τῇ πηγῇ.

With the accusative:

    To, upon, at. Jn. 6.16, κατέβησαν οἱ μαθηταὶ αὐτοῦ ἐπὶ τὴν θάλασσαν, his disciples came down to the sea. Jn. 7.30, ἐπ'αὐτόν. Jn. 8.59, ἐπ'αὐτόν.

In compound:

    a. Upon (place, superintendence). Jn. 7.30, οὐδεὶς ἐπέβαλεν ἐπ'αὐτὸν τὴν χεῖρα, no one put his hand upon him. Jn. 3.12, τὰ ἐπίγεια Ac. 20.28, ἐπισκόπους.

    b. Perfective. Mt. 11.27, οὐδεὶς ἐπιγινώσκε τὸν υἱὸν εἰ μὴ ὁ πατήρ, οὐδὲ τὸν πατέρα τις ἐπιγινώσκει εἰ μὴ ὁ υἱός, no one fully knows the Son except the Father, nor does anyone fully know the Father except the Son. Ro. 10.2, κατ'ἐπίγνωσιν.

Note: Various other related meanings for
ἐπί will also be found.

10. κατά (opposite of ἀνά, down)

With the genitive:

a. Against. Lk. 11.23, ʽΟ μὴ ὢν μετ'ἐμοῦ
κατ' ἐμοῦ ἐστιν, He who is not with
me is against me. Jn. 19.11, κατ'ἐμοῦ.

b. By (in oaths). Heb. 6.13, ἐπεὶ κατ'
οὐδενὸς εἶχεν μείζονος ὀμόσαι,
ὤμοσεν καθ'ἑαυτου,
take oath by no one greater, he took
oath by himself. Mt. 26.63, κατὰ τοῦ
θεοῦ.

c. Down, throughout. Lk. 8.33, ὥρμησεν ἡ
ἀγέλη κατὰ τοῦ κρημνοῦ, the herd
rushed down the slope. Lk. 4.14, καθ'
ὅλης τῆς περιχώρου.

With the accusative:

a. According to. Jn. 18.31, κατὰ τὸν νόμον
ὑμῶν κρίνατε αὐτόν, judge him
according to your law. Jn. 2.6, κατὰ
τὸν καθαρισμόν.

b. By (distributively). Lk. 22.53, καθ'ἡμέραν,
day by day. Jn. 21.25, καθ'ἕν.
Jn. 10.3, κατ'ὄνομα.

In compound:

a. Down. Jn. 1.32, τεθέαμαι τὸ πνεῦμα
καταβαῖνον, I beheld the Spirit coming down. Jn. 17.24, καταβολῆς.

b. Against. Jn. 18.29, τίνα κατηγορίαν
φέρετε τοῦ ἀνθρώπου τούτου; What
accusation do you bring against this
man? Mk. 14.60, καταμαρτυροῦσιν.

c. Intensive use. Jn. 2.17, ὁ ζῆλος τοῦ
οἴκου σου καταφάγεταί με, The zeal
of thy house will consume me. Jn. 1.5,
κατέλαβεν.

11. μετά

With the genitive:
With. Jn. 3.2, ἐὰν μὴ ᾖ ὁ θεὸς μετ'αὐτοῦ,
unless God be with him. Jn. 3.25, μετὰ
Ἰουδαίου.

With the accusative:
After. Jn. 13.7, γνώσῃ δὲ μετὰ ταῦτα,
but you will know after these things. Jn.
13.27, μετὰ τὸ ψωμίον.

In compound:
a. Change. Mk. 9.2, μετεμορφώθη, he
was transfigured. Jn. 5.24, μετα-
βέβηκεν.
b. With. Ac. 2.46, μετελάμβανον τροφῆς,
they were partaking of food. I Cor.
10.21, μετέχειν.

12. παρά (general meaning, alongside of)

With the genitive:
From beside, from. Jn. 1.6, Ἐγένετο
ἄνθρωπος, ἀπεσταλμένος παρὰ θεοῦ,
there came a man, sent from God. Jn.
4.9, παρ'ἐμοῦ.

With the dative:
Beside, with (generally at rest). Jn. 1.39,
παρ'αὐτῷ ἔμειναν, they remained
with him. Jn. 17.5, παρὰ σεαυτῷ . . .
παρὰ σοί.

With the accusative:
a. Alongside of, at (generally motion).
Mt. 15.29, ὁ Ἰησοῦς ἦλθεν παρὰ τὴν
θάλασσαν τῆς Γαλιλαίας, Jesus passed
along the sea of Galilee. Mt. 15.30, παρὰ
τοὺς πόδας αὐτοῦ.
b. Beyond, above. Lk. 3.13, Μηδὲν πλέον
παρὰ τὸ διατεταγμένον ὑμῖν
πράσσετε, Exact nothing above what
is commanded you. Lk. 13.2, παρὰ

πάντας τοὺς Γαλιλαίους.

c. __Contrary to.__ Ro. 11.24, παρὰ φύσιν,
contrary to nature. Ro. 16.17, παρὰ τὴν
διδαχήν.

In compound:
a. __Aside, amiss.__ Ac. 23.3, παρανομῶν,
acting contrary to law. Mt. 15.2,
·παραβαίνουσιν.
b. __Alongside of, by.__ Jn. 18.22,
εἷς παρεστηκὼς τῶν ὑπηρετῶν, one
of the officers who was standing by. Jn.
14.16, ἄλλον Παράκλητον.

13. περί (general meaning, __about__)

With the genitive:
__About, concerning.__ Jn. 15.26, ἐκεῖνος μαρτυ-
ρήσει περὶ ἐμοῦ, that one will tes-
tify concerning me. Jn. 16.8, περὶ ἁμαρτίας
καὶ περὶ δικαιοσύνης καὶ περὶ κρίσεως.

With the accusative:
__About, around.__ Mt. 18.6, περὶ τὸν τράχηλον
αὐτοῦ, around his neck. Mt.
20.3, περὶ τρίτην ὥραν.

In compound:
a. __Around.__ Jn. 11.42, διὰ τὸν ὄχλον τὸν
περιεστῶτα, on account of the crowd
which is standing around. Jn. 19.2,
περιέβαλον.
b. __Intensive use.__ Lk. 18.23, περίλυπος
ἐγενήθη, he became very grieved.
I Th. 4.15, οἱ περιλειπόμενοι.

14. πρό (general meaning, __before__)

With the genitive:
a. __Before__ (of time). Jn. 1.48, Πρὸ τοῦ σε
Φίλιππον φωνῆσαι, Before Philip
called you. Jn. 11.55, πρὸ τοῦ πάσχα.

b. __Before, in front of__ (of place). Ac. 12.6,
φυλακές τε πρὸ τῆς θύρας, and guards

42

in front of the door. Acts 12.14, πρὸ τοῦ
πυλῶνος.

    c. Before, above (of preference or superiority).
        Ja. 5.12, πρὸ πάντων, above (more im-
        portant than) all things. I Pe. 4.8, πρὸ
        πάντων.

In compound:
    a. Before, forth (of place). Mt. 26.32, προ-
        άξω ὑμᾶς, I shall go before you. Mk.
        14.68, εἰς τὸ προαύλιον.

    b. Beforehand (of time). Mk. 13.11, μὴ προ-
        μεριμνᾶτε, do not be anxious be-
        forehand. Mk. 14.8, προέλαβεν.

15. πρός (general meaning, to, opposite of ἀπό)
With the dative:
    At. Jn. 20.11, Μαρία δὲ εἰστήκει πρὸς
    τῷ μνημείῳ, but Mary stood at the tomb.
    Jn. 20.12, ἕνα πρὸς τῇ κεφαλῇ καὶ
    ἕνα πρὸς τοῖς ποσίν.

With the accusative:
    a. to, toward. Jn. 1.19, ἀπέστειλαν πρὸς
        αὐτὸν οἱ Ἰουδαῖοι, the Jews sent to
        him. Jn. 1.29, πρὸς αὐτόν.

    b. To (equivalent of indirect object). Jn. 2.3,
        λέγει ἡ μήτηρ τοῦ Ἰησοῦ πρὸς αὐτόν,
        the mother of Jesus said to him. Jn. 6.28,
        εἶπον οὖν πρὸς αὐτόν.

    c. At, with, in the presence of. Jn. 1.1, ὁ
        λόγος ἦν πρὸς τὸν θεόν, the Word
        was in the presence of God. Jn. 11.32,
        πρὸς τοὺς πόδας.
    d. Pertaining to, He. 1.7, πρὸς μὲν τοὺς
        ἀγγέλους, with reference to the angels.
        He. 5.1, τὰ πρὸς τὸν θεόν.

e. For the purpose of. Ro. 3.26 πρὸς τὴν
ἔνδειξιν της δικαιοσύνης αὐτοῦ,
for the purpose of showing his righteousness. Mt. 6.1, πρὸς τὸ θεαθῆναι
αὐτοῖς.

In compound:
a. To, toward . Jn. 12.21, οὗτοι οὖν προσ-
ῆλθον Φιλίππῳ, Now these men
came to Philip. Jn. 16.2, προσφέρειν.
b. In addition. Lk. 3.20, προσέθηκεν καὶ
τοῦτο ἐπὶ πᾶσιν, he added this also
to all (the rest). Lk. 19.16,
προσηργάσατο.

16. σύν (general meaning, with)

With the dative:
With, together with. Jn. 12.2, ὁ δὲ Λάζαρος
εἷς ἦν ἐκ τῶν ἀνακειμένων σὺν
αὐτῷ, and Lazarus was one of those who
were at table with him. Jn. 18.1, σὺν τοῖς
μαθηταῖς αὐτοῦ.

In compound:
Together, together with. Jn. 11.16, τοῖς συμ-
μαθηταῖς, to the fellow-disciples.
Jn. 6.22, συνεισῆλθεν.

17. ὑπέρ (general meaning, over, opposite of ὑπό)

With the genitive:
a. In behalf of, for the sake of. Jn. 13.38,
τὴν ψυχήν σου ὑπὲρ ἐμοῦ θήσεις;
Will you lay down your life for my
sake? Jn. 15.13, ὑπὲρ τῶν φίλων
αὐτοῦ.
b. Concerning, in reference to. II Cor.
5.12, ἀφορμὴν διδόντες ὑμῖν καυχή-
ματος ὑπὲρ ἡμων, giving you an
occasion of boasting concerning us.
II Co. 1.7, ὑπὲρ ὑμῶν.

With the accusative:

- a. Above, beyond (superiority). Mt. 10.
  24, Οὐκ ἔστιν μαθητὴς ὑπὲρ τὸν δι-
  δάσκαλον, A disciple is not above
  his teacher. Eph. 1.22, ὑπὲρ πάντα.

- b. Above, more than (excess). Mt. 10.37, ὁ
  φιλῶν πατέρα ἤ μητέρα ὑπὲρ ἐμέ, He
  who loves father or mother more
  than me. Ac. 26.13, ὑπὲρ τὴν λαμπρό-
  τητα τοῦ ἡλίου.

In compound:

Over, above. Ac. 17.30, τοὺς . . . χρόνους
τῆς ἀγνοίας ὑπεριδών, having
overlooked the times of ignorance. Ro.
8.37, ὑπερνικῶμεν.

18. ὑπό (general meaning, under, opposite of ὑπέρ)

With the genitive:

By (agency). Lk. 21.24, Ἱερουσαλὴμ ἔσται
πατουμένη ὑπὸ ἐθνῶν, Jerusalem
shall be trodden down by Gentiles. Jn.
14.21, ὑπὸ τοῦ πατρός μου.

With the accusative:

Under. Ro. 6.14, οὐ γάρ ἐστε ὑπὸ νόμον
ἀλλὰ ὑπὸ χάριν, for you are not under
law but under grace. Jn. 1.48, ὑπὸ τὴν
συκῆν.

In compound:

- a. Under (place). Lk. 21.19, ἐν τῇ ὑπο-
  μονῇ ὑμῶν, in your patience (i.e.,
  remaining under). Jn. 1.27, τοῦ
  ὑποδήματος.

- b. Under (subjection). Ro. 3.19, Ἵνα . . .
  ὑπόδικος γένηται πᾶς ὁ κόσμος, in
  order that . . . all the world might
  become subject to judgment. Ro. 1.5, εἰς
  ὑπακοήν.

45

B. Exceptions to basic rules of usage

1. In some instances, the "perfective" or "intensive" use of a compounded preposition has lost its intensive force and differs little from the meaning of the uncompounded form. E.g., cf. ἐρωτάω and ἐπερωτάω, ὄλλυμι and ἀπόλλυμι.

2. Prepositional phrases are sometimes used to express the same meaning as a pure case. E.g., compare ἐκ τῶν μαθητῶν αὐτοῦ δύο two of his disciples (Jn. 1.35), and the partitive genitive (Jn. 2.11), ἀρχὴν τῶν σημείων. ἐν σαββάτῳ, on a sabbath (Jn. 5.16), and the dative of time (Jn. 6. 54), τῇ ἐσχάτῃ ἡμέρᾳ. λέγει ἡ μήτηρ τοῦ Ιησοῦ πρὸς αὐτόν , the mother of Jesus said to him (Jn. 2.3), the dative of indirect object (Jn. 1.25), εἶπαν αὐτῷ.

3. Some prepositions are sometimes apparently interchanged with others with little or no difference in meaning. Each passage must, however, be studied separately in such cases to determine whether or not a difference in meaning is intended. Gr #308-14
E.g., ἀπὸ τῶν καρπῶν αὐτῶν (Mt. 7.16), ἐκ τοῦ ἰδίου καρποῦ (Lk. 6.44).
E.g., (possibly) πρὸς τὴν ἔνδειξιν τῆς δικαιοσύνης αὐτοῦ and εἰς τὸ εἶναι αὐτὸν δίκαιον (Ro. 3.26).
E.g., διὰ ποῖον αὐτῶν ἔργον and περὶ καλοῦ ἔργου . . . περὶ βλασφημίας (Jn. 10.32, 33).
Other examples may also be found.

C. Some adverbs, especially adverbs of place, may be used as prepositions. Almost all of them take the genitive case. Gr #133, 400
E.g., Jn. 1.26, μέσος ὑμῶν.

D. If a preposition is repeated before each of a
   series of nouns, each is to be considered separately; if not repeated, they are to be considered together. (Cf. Granville Sharp's rule of
   the definite article) Mt. 22.37, ἐν ὅλῃ τῇ καρδίᾳ
   σου καὶ ἐν ὅλῃ τῇ ψυχῇ σου καὶ ἐν ὅλῃ τῇ
   διανοίᾳ σου, but II Th. 2.9, ἐν πάσῃ δυνάμει
   καὶ σημείοις καὶ τέρασιν ψεύδους.

E. A verb compounded with a preposition may take
   a predicate in one of the following forms: (Gr
   #314, note)

   1. The case required by the simple verb.
      Mt. 21.41, οἵτινες ἀποδώσουσιν
      αὐτῷ τοὺς καρπούς.

   2. A prepositional phrase using the same or a
      similar preposition as that which is com-
      pounded, the prepositonal phrase taking its
      normal case. Jn. 9.15, πηλὸν ἐπέθηκέν
      μου ἐπὶ τοὺς ὀφθαλμούς.

   3. The case required by the compounded prep-
      osition, but without repeating the preposi-
      tion. Mt. 13.1, ἐξελθὼν ὁ Ἰησοῦς
      τῆς οἰκίας. Ga. 2.19, συνεσταύ-
      ρωμαι Χριστῷ.

IV. ADJECTIVES
    Gr #315-31

   A. Greek sometimes uses an adjective where Eng-
      lish requires an adverb. Ac. 12.10, ἥτις αὐτο-
      μάτη ἠνοίγη αὐτοῖς, which opened to them
      automatically.

   B. Constructions forming comparison:

      1. Genitive of comparison
         The second member of the comparison is
         placed in the genitive case. Jn. 8.53, μὴ σὺ
         μείζων εἶ τοῦ πατρὸς ἡμῶν Ἀβραάμ; Are

you greater than our __father__ Abraham? Jn.
5.36, Ἐγὼ δὲ ἔχω τὴν μαρτυρίαν μείζω
τοῦ Ἰωάννου.

2. The second member of the comparison may
    be placed in the same case as that of the
    first member, joined by ἤ, "than." Jn. 4.1,
    Ἰησοῦς πλείονας μαθητὰς ποιεῖ καὶ
    βαπτίζει ἤ Ἰωάννης, __Jesus__ was making and
    baptizing more disciples than __John__. Jn. 3.
    19, ἠγάπησαν οἱ ἄνθρωποι μᾶλλον τὸ
    σκότος ἤ τὸ φῶς.

3. The second member of the comparison is
    sometimes placed in a prepositional phrase,
    ὑπέρ with the accusative or παρά with the
    accusative. Lk. 16.8, οἱ υἱοὶ τοῦ αἰῶνος
    τούτου φρονιμώτεροι ὑπὲρ τοὺς υἱοὺς τοῦ
    φωτός,   the sons of this age are wiser
    __than__ the sons of light. He. 11.4, πλείονα
    θυσίαν Ἄβελ παρὰ Κάιν προσήνεγκεν.

C. The comparative degree is apparently sometimes
    used where English requires the superlative.
    I Co. 13.13, μείζων δὲ τούτων ἡ ἀγάπη, but the
    __greatest__ of these (three) is love. Mt. 18.1, τίς
    ἄρα μείζων ἐστὶν ἐν τῇ βασιλείᾳ τῶν
    οὐρανῶν;

V. PRONOUNS
    Gr #332-52

    Special notes on relative pronouns

    Some exceptions to normal syntax

A. When the antecedent of a relative pronoun is a
    pronoun or some other easily understood word
    such as "person," "time," etc., the antecedent
    is ordinarily omitted. Jn. 18.26, συγγενὴς ὢν οὗ
    ἀπέκοψεν Πέτρος τὸ ὠτίον, being a kinsman
    of __him__ whose ear Peter cut off. Jn. 5.21,
    ὁ υἱὸς οὓς θέλει ζωοποιεῖ.

B. The relative pronoun may be attracted to the <u>case</u>
    of its antecedent. Jn. 15.20, μνημονεύετε τοῦ
    λόγου οὗ ἐγὼ εἶπον ὑμῖν, Remember the word
    <u>which</u> (properly ὅν) I said to you. Jn. 4.14, ἐκ
    τοῦ ὕδατος οὗ (properly ὅ) ἐγὼ δώσω αὐτῷ.

    1. If the omission of the antecedent leaves a
        dangling preposition or other incomplete
        construction, the relative pronoun <u>must</u>
        take the place and case of the antecedent.
        Jn. 7.31, μὴ πλείονα σημεῖα ποιήσει ὧν
        οὗτος ἐποίησεν; will he do more miracles
        <u>than</u> <u>the</u> <u>ones</u> <u>which</u> (i.e., ποιήσει τῶν ση-
        μείων ἃ) this man has done? Jn. 17.9, ἐγὼ
        ἐρωτῶ . . . περὶ ὧν δέδωκάς μοι,
        I ask . . . concerning <u>the</u> <u>people</u> whom (i.e.,
        περὶ τῶν ἀνθρώπων οὓς) thou hast given
        me. He. 5.8, ἔμαθεν ἀφ᾽ ὧν ἔπαθεν
        τὴν ὑπακοήν.
    2. The relative pronoun sometimes replaces, and
        takes the case of, the article of its antecedent.
        Jn. 11.6, ἔμεινεν ἐν ᾧ ἦν τόπῳ (i.e.,
        ἐν τῷ τόπῳ ἐν ᾧ ἦν), he remained in
        the place in which he was. Jn. 9.14, ἐν
        ᾗ ἡμέρᾳ.

C. Occasionally, the <u>antecedent</u> is attracted to the case
    of the relative pronoun. I Co. 10.16, τὸν ἄρτον ὃν
    κλῶμεν, οὐχὶ κοινωνία τοῦ σώματος τοῦ Χρισ-
    τοῦ ἐστιν; Is not <u>the</u> <u>bread</u> (properly ἄρτος)
    which we break a sharing in the body of Christ? Mk.
    6.16, ὃν ἐγὼ ἀπεκεφάλισα Ἰωάννην (pro-
    perly Ἰωάννης), οὗτος ἠγέρθη.

D. The relative pronoun sometimes takes the <u>gender</u> of
    its predicate instead of its antecedent, when the pre-
    dicate is actually an explanation of the antecedent.
    Mk. 15.16, ἔσω τῆς αὐλῆς, ὅ ἐστιν πραιτώριον,
    inside the hall, which is the praetorium. Eph. 6.17,
    τὴν μάχαιραν . . . ὅ ἐστιν ῥῆμα θεοῦ.

E. The neuter relative pronoun is sometimes used as an adverb.

1. ὅ "whereas." Ro. 6.10, ὃ γὰρ ἀπέθανεν . . . ὃ δὲ ζῇ, For whereas he died . . . and whereas he lives. Ga. 2.20, ὃ δὲ νῦν ζῶ.

2. οὗ "where." Lk. 4.16, Καὶ ἦλθεν εἰς Ναζαρά, οὗ ἦν τεθραμμένος, And he came into Nazareth, where he had been brought up. Lk. 4.17, τὸν τόπον οὗ ἦν γεγραμμένον.

F. The pronoun αὐτός is sometimes used redundantly with a relative pronoun. Mk. 7.25, γυνὴ . . . ἧς εἶχεν τὸ θυγάτριον αὐτῆς, a woman . . . whose daughter (of whom the daughter of her). Jn. 1.27, οὗ οὐκ εἰμὶ ἐγὼ ἄξιος ἵνα λύσω αὐτοῦ τόν ἱμάντα τοῦ ὑποδήματος.

VI. VERBS

Bu; Gr #353-97; DM 155-233

A. Uses of moods. Bu 73-81

1. Indicative: mood of fact. Jn. 1.14, ὁ λόγος σάρξ ἐγένετο, the Word became flesh. Jn. 1.14, ἐσκήνωσεν.

2. Imperative: mood of command.
Used in commands, entreaties, prayers, etc., both affirmative and negative (except for the negative form with the aorist tense --see subjunctive). Jn. 17.11, πάτερ ἅγιε, τήρησον αὐτούς, Holy Father, keep them. Jn. 5.14, μηκέτι ἁμάρτανε, Sin no longer. Jn. 16.24, αἰτεῖτε.

3. Subjunctive: mood of contingency.

a. Hortatory subjunctive. Used in exhortations, first person plural. Jn. 19.24,

μὴ σχίσωμεν αὐτόν, let us not
divide it. Jn. 11.16, ἄγωμεν.

b. Deliberative questions, real or rhetorical. Deal with what is a) desirable,
b) possible, or c) necessary. Jn. 6.28,
τί ποιῶμεν; What should we do?
Jn. 19.15, τὸν βασιλέα ὑμῶν σταυρώσω;

c. The aorist subjunctive with the double
negative οὐ μή is used as a declarative future. Jn. 6.35, ὁ ἐρχόμενος πρὸς
ἐμὲ οὐ μὴ πεινάσῃ, He who comes
to me will by no means hunger. Jn. 6.37,
οὐ μὴ ἐκβάλω.

d. The aorist subjunctive (with μή) is used
instead of the aorist imperative to express a simple prohibition (negative
command with the aorist tense). Lk. 21.8,
μὴ πλανηθῆτε . . . μὴ πορευθῆτε
ὀπίσω αὐτῶν, do not be deceived . . .
do not go after them. Jn. 3.7, μὴ
θαυμάσῃς.

e. In dependent clauses of contingency.
E.g., Jn. 1.8, ἵνα μαρτυρήσῃ, in order
that he might testify. Jn. 3.12, ἐὰν
εἴπω.

4. Optative: mood of hope. (Rare in N. T.) E.g.,
to express a wish or prayer. 1 Th. 5.23,
Αὐτὸς δὲ ὁ θεὸς τῆς εἰρήνης ἁγιάσαι
ὑμᾶς ὁλοτελεῖς, May the God of peace himself make you completely holy. Ro. 3. 4,
μὴ γένοιτο.

B. Tense-aspects of the indicative mood. Bu 6-45; Gr #360-70

Outline of tenses of the indicative mood (Gr #65)

TIME OF ACTION

KIND OF ACTION	Present	Past	Future
Continued	γράφω (Present tense) I am writing	ἔγραφον (Imperfect tense) I was writing	γράψω (Future tense) I shall be writing
Undefined or Simple	γράφω (Present tense) I write	ἔγραψα (Aorist tense) I wrote	γράψω (Future tense) I shall write
Perfective (With state resulting)	γέγραφα (Perfect tense) I am in a condition resulting from having written	ἐγεγράμμην (Pluperfect tense) I was in a condition resulting from having written previously	ἔσομαι γεγραφώς (Future perfect tense) I shall be in a condition resulting from having written previously

1. Present

a. Present action* in progress or repeated. Jn. 1.48, πόθεν με γινώσκεις; From where do you know me? Jn. 1.50, πιστεύεις.

*Where the word "action" is used in this outline, the word "state" should be substituted if the verb is a verb of state instead of action.

b. Simple event in present time. Jn. 3.3, ἀμ
ἀμὴν λέγω σοι, Truly, truly I say
to you. Jn. 4.9, αἰτεις.

c. Gnomic present: customary action or
general truth. Jn. 2.10, πᾶς ἄνθρωπο
πρῶτον τὸν καλὸν οἶνον τίθησιν,
Every man (customarily) sets out the
good wine first. Jn. 3.8, τὸ πνευμα.
πνει.

d. Conative present: tendency or attempt
in present time. Ga. 5.4, οἵτινες ἐν
νόμῳ δικαιουσθε, you who are
attempting to be justified by law. Jn.
10.32, λιθάζετε.

e. Historic present: for vivid description
of past event. Jn. 1.29, Τῇ ἐπαύριον
βλέπει τὸν Ἰησοῦν, On the next day
saw Jesus. Jn. 1.29, λέγει.

f. Futuristic present: the present used for
the future. Jn. 14.2, πορεύομαι ἑτο
τόπον ὑμιν, I am going (i.e.,
I am going to go) to prepare a place
for you. Jn. 14.3, πάλιν ἔρχομαι.

g. Past action continuing into the present.
(Requires a specific phrase to show
the past aspect). Lk. 15.29, τοσαυτα
δουλεύω σοι, for so many years
I have been serving you. Jn. 14.9,
τοσοῦτον χρόνον μεθ'ὑμῶν εἰμι.

2. Imperfect

a. Action in progress (or state existing) in
past time. Jn. 2.25, αὐτὸς γὰρ ἐγί
τί ἦν ἐν τῳ ἀνθρώπῳ, for he
himself knew (continually) what was in
man. Jn. 11.36, ἐφίλει.

b. Action repeated in past time. Jn. 5.18, οὐ
μόνον ἔλυεν τὸ σάββατον, ἀλλὰ καὶ
πατέρα ἴδιον ἔλεγεν τὸν θεόν, he
not only was (repeatedly) breaking the
sabbath, but also was (more than once)
calling God his own father. Jn. 2.23,
τὰ σημεῖα ἃ ἐποίει.

c. Customary action in past time. Ac. 3.2
ὃν ἐτίθουν καθ' ἡμέραν, whom they
were accustomed to place daily. Mk.
15.6, ἀπέλυεν.

d. <u>Action</u> begun in past time. (Cf. aorist
of beginning of a <u>state</u>.) Lk. 5.6,
διερρήσσετο δὲ τὰ δίκτυα αὐτῶν, and
their nets began to break. Jn. 13.22,
ἔβλεπον εἰς ἀλλήλους οἱ μαθηταί.

e. Intention, or action attempted , but not
carried out, in past time. Ac. 7.26, συν-
ήλλασσεν αὐτούς, he attempted to
reconcile them.

f. Impossible, impractical, or hesitant
wish. Ro. 9.3, ηὐχόμην γὰρ ἀνάθεμα
.εἶναι αὐτὸς ἐγὼ ἀπὸ τοῦ Χριστοῦ
ὑπὲρ τῶν ἀδελφῶν μου, For I myself
could pray to be accursed from Christ for
the sake of my brothers (recognizing
the impossibility of God's granting
such a wish). Lk. 15.16, ἐπεθύμει γεμίσαι
τὴν κοιλίαν αὐτοῦ ἐκ τῶν κερατίων
ὧν ἤσθιον οἱ χοῖροι, Phlm. 13,
ὃν ἐγὼ ἐβουλόμην πρὸς ἐμαυτὸν
κατέχειν.

3. <u>Aorist</u>

a. Action completed in past time--
considered in its entirety, or as a
single fact. Jn. 1.11, οἱ ἴδιοι αὐτὸν οὐ
παρέλαβον, his own people did not

receive him. Jn. 1.12, ἔδωκεν.

b. Inceptive--the beginning of a state.
(Cf. imperfect of beginning of an action.) Lk. 15.32, ὁ ἀδελφός σου οὗτος
νεκρὸς ἦν καὶ ἔζησεν, this your
brother was dead and has come to life.
Ac. 7.60, ἐκοιμήθη.

c. Epistolary--in letters, to refer to what
will be a past action when the letter is
read although it is not past when the
letter is being written. Ph. 2.28, ἔπεμψα
αὐτόν,   I have sent him (with
this letter). Ga. 6.11, ῎Ιδετε πηλίκοις
ὑμῖν γράμμασιν ἔγραψα τῇ ἐμῇ χειρί
(if referring to the letters of this very
sentence).

d. Gnomic--general or proverbial truth
(less common than gnomic present).
I Pe. 1.24, ἐξηράνθη ὁ χόρτος, καὶ
τὸ ἄνθος ἐξέπεσεν, the grass withers and
the flower falls off (each season). Jn.
15.6, ἐβλήθη . . . ἐξηράνθη.

4. Future

a. Undefined or simple action in future
time. Jn. 14.26, τὸ πνεῦμα τὸ ἅγιον
ὁ πέμψει ὁ πατήρ, the Holy Spirit,
whom the Father will send. Jn. 14.3,
παραλήμψομαι.

b. Action in progress in future time. Jn.
14.30, οὐκέτι πόλλα λαλήσω μεθ᾽ὑμῶν,
No longer shall I be speaking much
with you. Jn. 14.12, ποιήσει.

c. Declarative future. Mt. 1.21, καλέσεις
τὸ ὄνομα αὐτοῦ ᾽Ιησοῦν, you
shall (you must) call his name Jesus.
Mt. 19.18-19, οὐ φονεύσεις, οὐ

μοιχεύσεις, οὐ κλέψεις, οὐ
ψευδομαρτυρήσεις, . . . καὶ
ἀγαπήσεις . . .

d. The future used for the aorist subjunctive, in various constructions where
the subjunctive is normally used. Jn.
6.68 (a deliberative question), κύριε, πρὸς
τίνα ἀπελευσόμεθα; Lord, to
whom could we go? Jn. 4.14, οὐ μὴ
διψήσει.

5. <u>Perfect</u> (present perfect)

Has a double emphasis: <u>present</u> <u>state</u> resulting from <u>past</u> <u>action</u>. (Is not merely
equivalent to the English perfect tense.)
Jn. 1.34, κἀγὼ ἑώρακα, καὶ μεμαρτύρηκα,
and I am in a condition resulting from
having seen, and I have borne an abiding
testimony. Jn. 2.10, τετήρηκας. Jn. 3. 13,
ἀναβέβηκεν.

6. <u>Pluperfect</u> (past perfect)

Has a double emphasis: <u>past</u> <u>state</u> resulting
from <u>previous</u> action. (Is not merely equivalent to the English pluperfect tense.) Jn.
1.24 (written periphrastically in this in-
stance), ἀπεσταλμένοι ἦσαν ἐκ τῶν
Φαρισαίων, they had been sent (i.e., they
were there with John as a result of having
been sent) from the Pharisees. Jn. 4.8, οἱ
γὰρ μαθηταὶ αὐτοῦ ἀπεληλύθεισαν εἰς τὴν
πόλιν, for his disciples were gone (i.e.,
they had gone and were still away) into the
city. Jn. 6.17, ἐγεγόνει.

7. <u>Future</u> <u>perfect</u> (rare in N. T., and occurring
only periphrastically)

Has a double emphasis: <u>future</u> <u>state</u> resulting from
action <u>prior</u> <u>to</u> <u>that</u> <u>state.</u> (Is not merely equivalent

to the English future perfect tense.) He. 2.13,
ἐγὼ ἔσομαι πεποιθὼς ἐπ'αὐτῷ, , I shall be
in a condition resulting from previously having
come to trust in him. Lk. 6.40, κατηρτισμένος
δὲ πᾶς ἔσται.

C. Tense-aspects of other moods (but see participle
separately, below)

1. <u>Present</u>. Denotes continuing or repeated
action. (The <u>time</u> of the action is deter-
mined by the leading verb or by the context.) Jn. 1.33, βαπτίζειν ἐν ὕδατι, to
baptize (habitually) in water. Jn. 1.43,
ἀκολούθει μοι.

2. <u>Aorist</u>. Denotes action conceived
as completed (at a time deter-
mined by the leading verb or by the context).
Jn. 1.7 (undefined action), οὗτος ἦλθεν εἰς
μαρτυρίαν, ἵνα μαρτυρήσῃ, This man
came for a testimony, in order that he
might testify. Jn. 2.7 (simple action),
γεμίσατε.

3. <u>Perfect</u>. Denotes a state (at a time deter-
mined by the leading verb or by the context) resulting from prior action. Jn. 17.19
(perfect passive subjunctive, written
periphrastically), ἵνα ὦσιν . . . ἡγι-
ασμένοι, in order that they may be in a
sanctified condition (resulting from prior
sanctifying). Mk. 4.39 (perfect passive
imperative), πεφίμωσο.

4. <u>Future</u> (rare in N. T.). Denotes action at a
time future to the leading verb. Ac. 23.30,
μηνυθείσης δέ μοι ἐπιβουλῆς εἰς τὸν
ἄνδρα ἔσεσθαι, but when a plot was revealed to
me which was to be (subsequently) against
the man. Ac. 24.15 (with the future tense
further reinforced by μέλλειν, as also in
11.28 and 27.10), μέλλειν ἔσεσθαι.

D. The infinitive: functions (Use of tenses, C. above.)

1. The anarthrous infinitive (without the article)

a. May express purpose. Jn. 4.15, ἵνα μὴ
διψῶ μηδὲ διέρχωμαι ἐνθάδε ἀντλεῖν,
in order that I may not thirst nor come
here to draw (i.e., for the purpose of
drawing) water. Jn. 1.33, βαπτίζειν.

b. May occasionally express result. Re.
5.5, ἐνίκησεν ὁ λέων ὁ ἐκ τῆς φυλῆς
Ἰούδα, ἡ ῥίζα Δαυίδ, ἀνοῖξαι τὸ
βιβλίον, the lion of the tribe of Judah,
the root of David, has conquered, with
the result that he can open the scroll.

c. May be used as a substantive: as a noun,
or translated as a substantive clause.

1) As a subject, object, in apposition,
etc. Jn. 1.43, ἠθέλησεν ἐξελθεῖν,
he wished to go out. Jn. 4.4,
διέρχεσθαι.

2) To define, limit, or give content of
nouns, adjectives, etc. Jn. 1.12,
ἔδωκεν αὐτοῖς ἐξουσίαν τέκνα θεοῦ
γενέσθαι, he gave them authority
to become children of God (i.e.,
the becoming children of God is
the content of the authority granted).
Jn. 13.10, χρείαν . . . νίψασθαι.

3) To express indirect discourse and
other indirect statements. Jn. 4.40,
ἠρώτων αὐτὸν μεῖναι παρ'
αὐτοῖς, they began asking him to
remain with them (i.e., indirect
form of the request, "Remain with
us").

2. The articular infinitive (with neuter article)

May usually be translated as an English gerund. Denotes a process (present tense), an event (aorist tense), or a state resulting from a prior action (perfect tense).

a. In various cases, expressing a normal meaning of the case. Phil. 1.21 (nominative, subject of understood verb), τὸ ζῆν Χριστὸς καὶ τὸ ἀποθανεῖν κέρδος, living is Christ and dying is gain. Lk. 1.9 (genitive, object of a verb which takes the genitive), ἔλαχε τοῦ θυμιᾶσαι, he was selected by lot to burn incense. Ac. 25.11 (accusative, object of a verb), οὐ παραιτοῦμαι τὸ ἀποθανεῖν.

b. Special uses in the genitive case

1) May express purpose. Mt. 2.13, μέλλει γὰρ Ἡρῴδης ζητεῖν τὸ παιδίον τοῦ ἀπολέσαι αὐτό, for Herod is about to seek the child for the purpose of destroying him. Mt. 3.13, τοῦ βαπτισθῆναι.

2) May occasionally express result. Ro. 7.3, ἐὰν δὲ ἀποθάνῃ ὁ ἀνήρ, ἐλευθέρα ἐστὶν ἀπὸ τοῦ νόμου, τοῦ μὴ εἶναι αὐτὴν μοιχαλίδα γενομένην ἀνδρὶ ἑτέρῳ, but if her husband dies, she is free from the law, with the result that she is not an adulteress if she becomes another man's. Mt. 21.32, τοῦ πιστευσαι.

3) May be used as a substantive in various ways; e.g.,

a) As subject: Ac. 27.1, ἐκρίθη τοῦ ἀποπλεῖν ἡμᾶς, it was decided that we should sail.

b) As object: Ac. 23.20, οἱ Ἰουδαῖοι
συνέθεντο τοῦ ἐρωτῆσαί σε.

c) To limit or explain a noun, verb,
or adjective. Lk. 2.6 (limiting
a noun), ἐπλήσθησαν αἱ ἡμέραι
τοῦ τεκεῖν αὐτήν, the days of
her giving birth (i.e., for her
to give birth) were fulfilled.
Lk. 9.51 (limiting verb), αὐτὸς τὸ
πρόσωπον ἐστήρισεν τοῦ
πορεύεσθαι εἰς Ἰερουσαλήμ,
he steadfastly set his face for
going (i.e., to go) into Jerusalem. Ac. 23.15 (limiting adjective), ἕτοιμοι . . . τοῦ ἀνελεῖν.

d) To express indirect discourse
and other indirect statements.
Ac. 15.20, ἀλλὰ ἐπιστεῖλαι
αὐτοῖς τοῦ ἀπέχεσθαι τῶν ἀλισ-
γημάτων τῶν εἰδώλων, but
to write to them to abstain from
the pollutions of idols (i.e., the
direct form would be, "Abstain
from . . .). Ac. 21.12, παρεκαλοῦμεν
. . . τοῦ μὴ ἀναβαίνειν.

c. In prepositional phrases

1) With various prepositions, following
the regular meaning for the preposition and case used. Jn. 2.24, διὰ τὸ
αὐτὸν γινώσκειν πάντας,   on
account of his knowing (i.e., because he knew) all people. Jn. 1. 48,
πρὸ τοῦ . . . φωνῆσαι.

2) Uses with εἰς and the accusative

a) May express purpose. Ro. 4.16, εἰς
τὸ εἶναι βεβαίαν τὴν ἐπ-
αγγελίαν, in order that the

promise might be guaranteed.
Ro. 7.4, εἰς τὸ γενέσθαι
ὑμᾶς ἑτέρῳ.

b) **May occasionally express result.**
I Th. 2.16, εἰς τὸ ἀναπληρῶσαι
αὐτῶν τὰς ἀμαρτίας, resulting
in filling up their sins. Ro. 1.20,
εἰς τὸ εἶναι αὐτοὺς
ἀναπολογήτους.

c) **May be used as a substantive ex-**
pression, as the predicate of a
verb or to express an indirect
statement, or to define or
limit a verb, adjective, noun.
Phil. 1.23 (predicate of a verb), τὴν
ἐπιθυμίαν ἔχων εἰς τὸ ἀνα-
λῦσαι, having the desire for
departing (i.e., to depart). II
Th. 2.1,2 (indirect exhortation),
ἐρωτῶμεν δὲ ὑμᾶς . . . εἰς τὸ
μὴ ταχέως σαλευθῆναι
But we ask you . . . that you not
quickly be shaken (i.e., in direct form,
"Do not quickly be shaken").

E. **The participle (Bu 163-77; Gr #393-97; DM 220-33)**

1. Uses of tenses of the participle. Bu 53-72

   a. Present. Bu 54-59

      1) Continuing or repeated action. Jn. 3.20,
      πᾶς γὰρ ὁ φαῦλα πράσσων, For
      everyone who makes a practice of
      evil things. Jn. 3.21, ὁ δὲ ποιῶν
      τὴν ἀλήθειαν.

      2) Action simultaneous to leading verb.
      Jn. 1.32, Τεθέαμαι τὸ πνεῦμα κατα-
      βαῖνον, I beheld the Spirit

61

(while it was) descending. Jn. 1. 47.

ἐρχόμενον.

3) Same action as leading verb. Jn. 1. 32,
ἐμαρτύρησεν Ἰωάννης λέγων,
John testified (by) saying. Jn. 1. 26,
λέγων.

4) To identify as a member of a class
(attributive participles only, commonly used substantively and
translated as a noun). Jn. 4. 37, ἄλλος
ἐστίν ὁ σπείρων, one is the
sower. Jn. 4. 37, ὁ θερίζων.

b. Aorist. Bu 59-70

1) Action conceived as a completed
event. Jn. 1. 33, ὁ πέμψας με . . .
εἶπεν he who sent me . . . said.
Jn. 18. 22, εἰπών.

2) Action antecedent to leading verb.
Jn. 5. 11, Ὁ ποιήσας με ὑγιῆ . . .
εἶπεν, He who made me well . . .
said (afterwards). Jn. 5. 13, ὁ
δὲ ἰαθεὶς οὐκ ᾔδει.

3) Same action as leading verb. Mt.
27. 4, Ἥμαρτον παραδοὺς αἷμα ἀθῷον,
I have sinned in betraying innocent
blood. Mt. 28. 5, ἀποκριθεὶς . . .
εἶπεν.

c. Future (rare). Bu 70-71
Expresses action future to leading verb.
Ac. 8. 27, ὃς ἐληλύθει προσκυνήσων,
who had come to worship (worshipping
subsequent to coming). Jn. 6. 64, ὁ παραδώσων. (May be expressed by the
present participle of μέλλω with the
infinitive of the required verb. Jn. 12. 4,
λέγει δὲ Ἰούδας . . . ὁ μέλλων

αὐτὸν παραδιδόναι, Judas,
. . . who was going to betray him (subsequently), said.

d. Perfect. Bu 71-72
Expresses a state resulting from completed action. Jn. 15.25, ὁ λόγος ὁ ἐν
τῷ νόμῳ αὐτῶν γεγραμμένος, the
word which stands written in their
law. Jn. 1.6, ἀπεσταλμένος.

2. Functions of the participle.

a. Adjectival

1) Includes all attributive participles
(For attributive and predicate pos-
ition, see above, Etymology VIII.
A, p. 13 .)

Attributive participles are either
definite (with article) or indefinite
(without article).

Attributive participles are either restrictive or non-restrictive.

a) Definite restrictive: Jn. 6.50, ὁ
ἄρτος ὁ . . . καταβαίνων,
the bread which comes down.
Jn. 4.11, τὸ ὕδωρ τὸ ζῶν.

b) Indefinite restrictive: Jn. 15.2,
πᾶν κλῆμα . . . μὴ φέρον
καρπόν, Every branch . . .
which does not bear fruit. Jn.
4.10, ὕδωρ ζῶν.

c) Definite non-restrictive: Jn. 7. 50,
Νικόδημος . . , ὁ ἐλθὼν πρὸς
αὐτὸν πρότερον, Nicodemus
. . , who had come to him previously. Jn. 1.29, ὁ ἀμνὸς τοῦ

θεοῦ ὁ αἴρων τὴν ἁμαρτίαν
του κόσμου.

d) Indefinite non-restrictive: Jn. 5. 2,
κολυμβήθρα, ἡ ἐπιλεγομένη
'Εβραιστὶ Βηθζαθά, πέντε στοὰς
ἔχουσα, a pool, which is called
in Hebrew Bethzatha, which has
five porticoes. Jn. 4.14, πηγή . . .
ἁλλομένου.

Restrictive participles may modify
an understood noun--i. e. , may
be used substantively.

Definite: Jn. 3.13, ὁ ἐκ τοῦ οὐρανοῦ
καταβάς , he who came down
from heaven. Jn. 2.14, τοὺς
πωλοῦντας.

Indefinite: Jn. 10.21, ταῦτα τὰ ῥήματα
οὐκ ἔστιν δαιμονιζομένου,
these are not the words of one who is
demon-possessed. Jn. 1.23, βοῶντος.

2) <u>Includes</u> <u>some</u> <u>predicate</u> <u>participles</u>

a) Primary predicates

(1) Participle used as a subject
complement--copulative and
other verbs. Modifies the
subject. Jn. 18.18, ἦν δὲ καὶ
ὁ Πέτρος μετ'αὐτῶν ἑστὼς καὶ
θερμαινόμενος, and
Peter also was with them,
standing and warming him-
self. Jn. 1.31, ἦλθον ἐγὼ
. . . βαπτίζων.

(2) Participles used in periphrastic tense formations. Jn.
3.24 (plup. pass. ind.), οὔπω

γὰρ ἦν βεβλημένος εἰς τὴν
φυλακὴν Ἰωάννης, for
John had not yet been cast
into prison. Jn. 3.28 (perf.
pass. ind.), ἀπεσταλμένος
εἰμί.

b) Secondary predicates
Predicate complement, modifying the object of a verb. Jn.
1.29, βλέπει τὸν Ἰησοῦν ἐρχόμενον, he sees Jesus com-
ing. Jn. 1.32, τεθέαμαι τὸ
πνεῦμα καταβαῖνον.

b. Adverbial
Includes all predicate participles except those above. Genitive absolute
participles are always adverbial predicate participles. Denote one or more
of the following:

1) Time. May be translated by English
temporal clause introduced by "while"
(if present tense), "after" (if aorist tense),
"when," etc. Jn. 6.59, Ταῦτα εἶπεν
. . . διδάσκων, These things he said
. . . while he was teaching. Jn. 4.54,
ἐλθών.

2) Condition. May be translated by English conditional clause introduced
by "if," etc. I Co. 11.29, μὴ δια-
κρίνων τὸ σῶμα, if he does not
discern the body. Ga. 6.9 μὴ
ἐκλυόμενοι.

3) Concession. May be translated by
English concessive clause introduced by "although," "even though,"
etc. Jn. 9.25, τυφλὸς ὤν, although I was blind. Jn. 12.37,
αὐτοῦ . . . πεποιηκότος.

4) Cause. May be translated by English causal clause introduced by "because," "for," "since," etc. Jn. 5.13, ὄχλου ὄντος ἐν τῷ τόπῳ, because a crowd was in the place. Jn. 11.51, ἀρχιερεὺς ὤν.

5) Purpose. May be translated by English purpose clause introduced by "in order that," etc. , or by English infinitive of purpose. (Future participles regularly denote purpose.) II Co. 1.23, φειδόμενος ὑμῶν, in order to spare you. Jn. 6.6, πειράζων αὐτόν.

6) Result (as distinguished from purpose). Mk. 7.13, ἀκυροῦντες τὸν λόγον τοῦ θεοῦ,   resulting in nullifying the word of God. Jn. 5.18, ἴσον ἑαυτὸν ποιῶν τῷ θεῷ.

7) Means. Used of the agent or instrument of an action. Mt. 6.27, τίς δὲ ἐξ ὑμῶν μεριμνῶν δύναται, who of you by being anxious is able . . . ? Jn. 20.31, πιστεύοντες.

8) Manner. Ac. 2.13, ἕτεροι δὲ διαχλευάζοντες ἔλεγον, but others mocking (i. e. , in a mocking manner) were saying. I Co. 9.26, ὡς οὐκ ἀέρα δέρων.

9) Attendant circumstance. Usually follows the leading verb; usually present tense. Describes a circumstance accompanying the leading verb. (Sometimes appears closely related to the participle used as subject complement or predicate complement, but those participles are more descriptive

of the noun modified, while the participle of attendant circumstance gives accompanying or attendant facts.)

Jn. 19.5, ἐξῆλθεν οὖν ὁ Ἰησοῦς ἔξω, φόρων τὸν ἀκάνθινον στέφανον, Then Jesus went outside, wearing the crown of thorns. Jn. 19.17, βαστάζων ἑαυτῷ τὸν σταυρὸν ἐξῆλθεν.

10) <u>Coordinate</u> <u>circumstance</u>. Normally precedes the leading verb in word order, normally is an aorist participle, and precedes the leading verb in time of action. Used (as is the English <u>present</u> participle in the English literary counterpart of this idiom) to describe an action <u>prior</u> to, <u>coordinate</u> in thought with, and of the <u>same</u> <u>mood</u> as the leading verb. May therefore be translated as a finite verb of the same mood and tense as the leading verb, connected with the leading verb by "and." Is to be distinguished from the temporal participle in its emphasis upon logically coordinate actions rather than upon subordinate temporal relationship. (More than one such participle may precede a leading verb.) Jn. 12.24, ἐὰν μὴ ὁ κόκκος τοῦ σίτου πεσὼν εἰς τὴν γῆν ἀποθάνῃ, unless the grain of wheat <u>fall</u> into the ground <u>and</u> die. Jn. 12.36, ἀπελθὼν ἐκρύβη, he <u>departed and</u> hid himself. Jn. 12.14, εὑρὼν . . . ἐκάθισεν.

11) <u>Apposition</u>. Same <u>action</u> as the leading verb. Jn. 1.32, ἐμαρτύρησεν Ἰωάννης λέγων, John testified saying. Jn. 4.31, λέγοντες.

VII. SUMMARY OF CONSTRUCTIONS

A. Time. DM 279 ff.

1. Definite time

   a. Time within which
      Genitive case. Jn. 3.2, οὗτος ἦλθεν . . .
      νυκτός,   This man came . . . dur-
      ing the night.

   b. Point of time

      1) Dative case. Jn. 2.1, τῇ ἡμέρᾳ τῇ
         τρίτῃ, on the third day.

      2) ἐν with the dative case. Jn. 1.1, Ἐν ἀρ-
         χῇ ἦν ὁ λόγος, In the beginning
         was the Word.

   c. Extent of time
      Accusative case. Jn. 4.40, ἔμεινεν ἐκεῖ
      δύο ἡμέρας,   he remained there
      for two days.

2. Relative time

   a. <u>Prior</u> to leading verb

      1) Prepositional phrase: μετά with the
         accusative. Jn. 4.43, Μετὰ δὲ τὰς δύο
         ἡμέρας,   And after the two days.

      2) Aorist participle (temporal). Jn. 16.8,
         ἐλθὼν ἐκεῖνος ἐλέγξει, when
         that one has come he will reprove.

      3) Clauses

         a) Actual time. Clauses introduced
            by "when" (ὅτε, ὡς, etc.)
            with the indicative mood. Jn.
            6.24, ὅτε οὖν εἶδεν ὁ ὄχλος,

When therefore the crowd saw.

b) Contingent time. Clauses introduced by "when (-ever)," etc.
(ὅταν,etc.) with the subjunctive mood. Jn. 4.25, ὅταν ἔλθῃ
ἐκεῖνος, when that one
comes.

b. Same time as leading verb

1) Prepositional phrase: ἐν with the
dative case. Lk. 24.15, ἐν τῷ ὁμιλ-
εῖν αὐτούς, while they were
talking (i.e., in their talking).

2) Present participle (temporal). Jn.
6.59, Ταῦτα εἶπεν . . . διδάσκων,
These things he said . . . while he
was teaching.

3) Clauses

a) Actual time. Clauses introduced
by "while" (ἕως, ὡς, etc.). Jn.9.4.,
ἡμᾶς δεῖ ἐργάζεσθαι . . . ἕως
ἡμέρα ἐστίν, It is necessary
for us to be working . . . while it is
day.

b) Contingent time. Clauses introduced by "while," etc. with
the subjunctive mood. Mt. 14.22,
καὶ προάγειν αὐτὸν εἰς τὸ
πέραν, ἕως οὗ ἀπολύσῃ τοὺς
ὄχλους,and to precede him to
the other side, while he dis-
missed the crowds.

c. Time subsequent to leading verb

1) Prepositional phrases:

a) ἕως with the genitive case. Lk.
23.44, σκότος ἐγένετο ἐφ'ὅλην
τὴν γῆν ἕως ὥρας ἐνάτης, darkness came upon all the earth
until the ninth hour.

b) πρό with the genitive case. Jn. 1.48,
πρό τοῦ σε Φίλιππον φωνῆσαι
. . . εἶδόν σε, Be-
fore Philip called you . . . I
saw you.

2) πρίν or πρίν ἤ with the infinitive.
Jn. 4.49, κατάβηθι πρὶν ἀποθανεῖν
τὸ παιδίον μου, come down before my child dies.

3) Future participle, or present participle of μέλλω with an infinitive.
Jn. 6.64, ᾔδει . . . ὁ Ἰησοῦς...
τίς ἐστιν ὁ παραδώσων αὐτόν, Jesus knew . . . who it was who
would betray him. Jn. 12.4, λέγει δὲ
Ἰούδας . . . ὁ μέλλων αὐτόν
παραδιδόναι, Judas . . . ,
who was going to betray him, said.

4) Clauses

a) Actual time. Clauses introduced
by "until" (ἕως, ἄχρι, etc.)
with the indicative mood. Jn.
9.18, οὐκ ἐπίστευσαν οὖν οἱ
Ἰουδαῖοι . . . ἕως ὅτου
ἐφώνησεν τοὺς γονεῖς αὐτοῦ,
The Jews therefore did not believe . . . until they had
called his parents.

b) Contingent time. Clauses introduced by "until" with the subjunctive mood. Lk. 21.24,
ἄχρι οὗ πληρωθῶσιν καιροὶ

ἐθνων, until the times of the
Gentiles are fulfilled.

B. **Cause.** DM 274-5; Bu 97-8

    1. Prepositional phrases

        a. ἀντί with the genitive. Eph. 5.31, ἀντί
        τούτου, Because of this.

        b. διά with the accusative. Jn. 2.24, διὰ τὸ
        αὐτὸν γινώσκειν πάντας, because
        of his knowing all people.

        c. χάριν with the genitive. I Jn. 3.12, χάριν
        τίνος; because of what?

    2. Participle. Jn. 5.13, ὄχλου ὄντος ἐν τῷ τόπῳ,
    because a crowd was in the place.

    3. Clauses introduced by γάρ, ὅτι, etc., Jn. 2.25,
    ὅτι οὐ χρείαν εἶχεν, because he did
    not have need.

C. **Condition.** DM 286-91; Gr #383; Bu 100-12

    1. Participle. Ga. 6.9, θερίσομεν μὴ ἐκ-
    λυόμενοι, we shall reap if we do not
    grow weary.

    2. Clauses

        a. Condition of fact. Actual condition in
        present or past. εἰ with the indicative.
        Jn. 3.12, εἰ τὰ ἐπίγεια εἶπον ὑμῖν,
        If I have told you earthly things.

        b. Condition of contingency. Future or
        general condition. ἐὰν with the sub-
        junctive. Jn. 3.12, πῶς ἐὰν εἴπω ὑμῖν τὰ
        ἐπουράνια πιστεύσετε; how
        will you believe if I should tell you the
        heavenly things?

c. Condition contrary to fact. εἰ with the
indicative (secondary tenses), sometimes
with ἄν in the apodosis. Jn. 11.21,
κύριε, εἰ ἦς ὧδε, οὐκ ἄν ἀπέθανεν
ὁ ἀδελφός μου, Lord, if you had been here
my brother would not have died.

D. Concession. DM 291-93; Bu 112-16
Similar in form to condition (above), but express
a contrary conclusion to a condition.

1. Participle. Jn. 9.25, τυφλὸς ὢν ἄρτι βλέπω,
although I was blind now I see.

2. Clauses

a. Actual concession. εἰ καί or εἰ with
the indicative (present or past tenses).
Lk. 18.4-5, εἰ καὶ τὸν θεὸν οὐ φοβοῦμαι
. . . ἐκδικήσω αὐτήν,   Although I do not fear God . . . I will
vindicate her.

b. Concession of certain or likely future.
Regarded not as a contingency but as a
foreseen fact. εἰ καί or εἰ with the
future indicative. Lk. 11.8, εἰ καὶ οὐ
δώσει αὐτῷ ἀναστὰς διὰ τὸ εἶναι φίλον
αὐτοῦ, διά γε τὴν ἀναίδειαν αὐτοῦ
ἐγερθεὶς δώσει αὐτῷ, although
he will not arise and give to him because he
is a friend. nevertheless because of his
importunity he will arise and give to him.

c. Concession of contingency. ἐὰν καί, καὶ
ἐάν   , or ἐάν with the subjunctive.
Jn. 11.25, ὁ πιστεύων εἰς ἐμὲ κἂν ἀποθάνῃ ζήσεται, he who believes in
me, even though he die, he shall live.

E. Purpose. Gr #384; DM 282-85; Bu (see index)

1. Prepositional phrase: εἰς (sometimes πρός)

72

with the accusative. Jn. 9.39, εἰς κρίμα,
For the purpose of judgment.

2. Participle. Jn. 6.6, τοῦτο δὲ ἔλεγεν πειράζων
αὐτόν,   But this he was saying for
the purpose of testing him.

3. Anarthrous infinitive. Jn. 1.33, ὁ πέμψας
με βαπτίζειν,   he who sent me to
baptize (i.e., for the purpose of baptizing).

4. Genitive case of the articular infinitive. Mt.
11.1, μετέβη ἐκεῖθεν τοῦ διδάσκειν καὶ
κηρύσσειν, he went away from there for the
purpose of teaching and preaching.

5. Clauses introduced by ἵνα, ὅπως, sometimes μή.
Jn. 3.16, ἵνα πᾶς ὁ πιστεύων εἰς αὐτὸν
μὴ ἀπόληται,   in order that everyone
who believes in him might not perish.

F. Result. DM 285-86; Bu (see index)

1. The regular expression for result: ὥστε with
the infinitive (twice in the New Testament
with the indicative). I Co. 13.2, κἂν ἔχω πᾶσαν
τὴν πίστιν ὥστε ὄρη μεθιστάναι, and
if I should have all faith, with the result
that I could remove mountains.

2. Expressions ordinarily not expressing result,
but occasionally denoting result as distinct
from purpose.

a. Participle. Jn. 5.18, πατέρα ἴδιον
ἔλεγεν τὸν θεόν, ἴσον ἑαυτὸν ποιῶν
τῷ θεῷ,   he was calling God his own
father, thereby making himself equal
to God.

b. Prepositional phrase: εἰς with the accusative. Ro. 1.20, εἰς τὸ εἶναι αὐτοὺς
ἀναπολογήτους,   with the result

73

that they are without excuse.

c. Anarthrous infinitive. Re. 5.5, ἐνίκησεν
ὁ λέων ὁ ἐκ τῆς φυλῆς 'Ιούδα, . . .
ἀνοῖξαι τὸ βιβλίον, the Lion who
is of the tribe of Judah . . . has conquered with the result that he can open
the scroll.

d. Genitive case of the articular infinitive.
Ro. 7.3, ἐὰν δὲ ἀποθάνῃ ὁ ἀνήρ,
ἐλευθέρα ἐστὶν ἀπὸ τοῦ νόμου, τοῦ
μὴ εἶναι αὐτὴν μοιχαλίδα γενομένην
ἀνδρὶ ἑτέρῳ, But if her husband dies, she is
free from the law, with the result that
she is not an adulteress if she becomes
another man's.

e. Clauses introduced by ἵνα or ὅπως . Jn.
9.2, ῥαββί, τίς ἥμαρτεν, . . .
ἵνα τυφλὸς γεννηθῇ; Rabbi, who sinned
. . . resulting in his being born blind?

G. Substantive expressions. DM 293-96

1. Direct discourse. Jn. 3.3, εἶπεν αὐτῷ,
ἀμὴν ἀμὴν .., he said to him, "Truly,
truly . . ."

2. Clauses (not causal) introduced by ὅτι. When
ὅτι means "that," the clause is the indirect
form of a statement in the indicative mood.
Preserves the tense and mood of the direct
statement. Jn. 1.34, μεμαρτύρηκα ὅτι οὗτός
ἐστιν ὁ υἱὸς τοῦ θεοῦ, I have testified that this is the Son of God.

3. Clauses (not purpose or result) introduced
by ἵνα. ὅπως, or μή . The indirect form of
statements whose direct form would be in
a mood other than the indicative; or a
clause defining, limiting, or giving the content of a noun, adjective, etc. Takes the

subjunctive mood (rarely, future indicative).
Jn. 4.47, ἠρώτα ἵνα καταβῇ καὶ ἰάσεται
αὐτοῦ τὸν υἱόν, he asked that he would come
down and heal his son. Jn. 1.27, οὐκ εἰμὶ
ἄξιος ἵνα λύσω αὐτοῦ τὸν ἱμάντα τοῦ ὑποδήματος, I am not worthy that I should
loose the thong of his sandal.

4. Anarthrous infinitive. Alternate form for
either ἵνα or ὅτι clauses (2. and 3.
above) for indirect statement. Jn. 21.25, οὐδ'
αὐτὸν οἶμαι τὸν κόσμον χωρήσειν τὰ γραφό-
μενα βιβλία, I think that not even the
world itself would have room for the books
which would be written. (Lit. . . . the
world itself not to have room for . . .)
Jn. 4.40, ἠρώτων αὐτὸν μεῖναι παρ'αὐτοῖς,
they were asking him to remain (i.e., were
asking that he remain) with them.

5. Genitive case of the articular infinitive. To
define or limit a noun, etc., similarly to
ἵνα clauses (3. above). Lk. 10.19, δέδωκα ὑμῖν
τὴν ἐξουσίαν τοῦ πατεῖν ἐπάνω ὄφεων,
I have given you the authority to tread upon
serpents.

6. Prepositional phrase: εἰς with the accusative. May be used in the sense of the predicate of a verb. II Th. 2.1-2, Ἐρωτῶμεν δὲ
ὑμᾶς . . . εἰς τὸ μὴ ταχέως σαλευθῆναι
ὑμᾶς, But we ask you . . . that you be not
quickly shaken. I Co. 15.45, ἐγένετο ὁ πρῶτος
ἄνθρωπος Ἀδὰμ εἰς ψυχὴν ζῶσαν,
The first man Adam became a living soul.

H. Questions. Ma 170-72
May be prefaced by οὐ if an affirmative answer
is expected, or by μή if a negative answer is
expected.

Are to be classified under each of the following
headings:

1. Real or rhetorical
   a. Real: asks for information
   b. Rhetorical: no answer required

2. Factual or deliberative

   a. Factual: deals with facts; indicative mood.
   b. Deliberative: deals with possibility, desirability, or necessity; subjunctive mood.

3. Direct or indirect
   Indirect questions normally preserve the tense, mood, and any interrogative word of the direct form of the question. When the direct form has no interrogative word, the indirect form is sometimes introduced by εἰ , "whether."

   Jn. 4.12, μὴ σὺ μείζων εἶ τοῦ πατρὸς ἡμῶν Ἰακώβ; You are not greater than our father Jacob, are you? (Real, factual, direct, expecting negative answer.)

   Jn. 12.49, αὐτός μοι ἐντολὴν δέδωκεν τί εἴπω, he has given me a commandment as to what I should speak (i.e., a commandment answering the implied question, "What should I speak?"). (Real, deliberative of desirability, indirect.)

VIII. SUGGESTIONS CONCERNING EXEGESIS

A. Additional items to observe

1. Words

   a. Background meaning (e.g., στέφανος, "victor's crown"; διάδημα, "king's crown")

   b. Prefixes, suffixes, etc. (e.g., ἀμφίβληστρον, fish-net, from βλη-, "throw," ἀμφι-, "around," -τρον, "instrument")

2. Agreement

   a. Case (e.g., the agreement of ποιμένα with Ἰησοῦν and not with θεός in Heb. 13.21 shows that it is "Jesus," not "God," who is "the great shepherd of the sheep")

   b. Gender (e.g., in Eph. 2.8 τοῦτο agrees in gender with neither "grace" nor "faith"; it is neuter and means "this whole condition," not "this faith" nor "this grace")

   c. Number (e.g., in He. 12.14, where both number and gender are involved: οὗ, "which," is singular and therefore cannot refer to both "peace" and "holiness," as if it were "apart from which things"; but it does agree in gender with "holiness," indicating "apart from holiness no one shall see the Lord.")

3. Emphasis

   a. A word standing first in its clause is usually emphatic. A subject or a verb commonly stand first, and are commonly the emphatic words of a clause. If some other word stands first, there is likely emphasis upon this word (e.g., the direct object θεὸν in the first clause of Jn. 1.18, οὕτως in Jn. 3.16, and ἀπὸ θεοῦ in Jn. 3.2)

b. A word standing out of its usual order is likely to be emphatic (e.g., a genitive preceding instead of following the word to which it refers, as θεοῦ thrice in Eph. 3.9).

c. Note use of emphatic words (e.g., ἐγώ , etc.) and of enclitics accented because of emphasis.

B. Suggestions concerning procedure

1. Clauses

a. If a dependent clause, what does it tell?

1) A noun clause tells "what" (what he said, what we saw, etc.). May be introduced by ὅτι, ἵνα, etc.

2) An adjectival clause tells "which one" and similar ideas (which man, whose house, etc.). Most are introduced by relative pronouns or relative adjectives (e.g., ὅς, ὅστις, ὅσος).

3) An adverbial clause gives most other qualifications--when, where, how, why, result, condition, etc. Introduced by subordinate conjunctions, relative adverbs, etc. (e.g., ὅτε, ὅπου, γάρ, εἰ).

b. An independent clause may be introduced by a conjunction of addition or contrast (e.g., "and," "but," "nevertheless"--καί, δέ, ἀλλά) or may have no introductory word.

2. Nouns

What is the use of its case?

What is the use of the article, or of the absence of article?

3. Pronouns

>What is its antecedent (i.e., to what word does it refer)?

>What type of pronoun is it and what, therefore, is its significance?

4. Adjectives and participles

>What does it modify?

>Is it in attributive or predicate position, and what, therefore, is its meaning?

5. Verbs

>What is the <u>use</u> of its mood (or, What is its <u>function</u> if it is a participle or an infinitive)?

>What is the <u>use</u> of its tense?

C. Special notes re: indirect forms

1. If <u>direct</u> discourse or similar direct statement is or would be in the <u>indicative</u> mood, its <u>indirect</u> form will then be expressed either by ὅτι with the indicative mood or by an infinitive; e.g., Jn. 1.34, Lk. 11.18 ἐκβαλλειν με.

2. If direct discourse or similar direct statement is or would be in the subjunctive, imperative, or optative mood, its indirect form will then be expressed either by ἵνα (sometimes ὅπως) with the subjunctive mood or by an infinitive; e.g., Jn. 4.47, Jn. 4.40.

3. An indirect question is commonly introduced by the same interrogative word which would introduce its direct form; e.g., τί in Jn. 2.25, πότε in Lk. 17.20.

4. Both in statements and in questions, the <u>indirect</u> form retains the tense which its <u>direct</u> form has or would have.

INDEX